RED ROAR
20 Years of Words

Niall Griffiths

Red Roar - 20 Years of Words

Niall Griffiths

All rights reserved. No part of this book may be reproduced, stored in a retrieval system or transmitted in any form or by any means electronic, mechanical, photocopying, recording or otherwise, without the prior permission of the publisher.

ISBN 9781903110201

First published in this edition 2015 by Wrecking Ball Press.

Copyright Niall Griffiths

Cover design by Owen Benwell

All rights reserved.

Supported by
Hull UK City of Culture 2017

RED ROAR – 20 YEARS OF WORDS

Ever since his first novel lit up the literary skies at the turn of the millennium, Niall Griffiths has been my favourite British writer by a country mile. At the time I read Grits I was living in a shared house very much like the one depicted in the book – a disparate community of bright minded waifs and strays brought together by disparate circumstance and a shared passion for hedonism under difficult circumstances. Like Colm and Liam and Mairead and Maggie, ours was a life scorched bright by a relentless succession of ecstatic highs and rendered dark by the resultant grubby comedowns. The characters in Grits and the turbo-charged prose that painted their inner and outer worlds in such vivid colours captivated me to such an extent that I fancied for one brief moment that Griffiths may have been peering through our window and taking notes.

The other works followed and I lapped them all up like a thirsty man kneeling at an oasis. To my mind, nobody else was documenting life in modern Britain with such an intense and unsparing eye for the telling detail. So much of the stuff offered up in the guise of new and vital modern writing was falling from my hands with a barely suppressed yawn. This, though, this was proper gear, the real deal. By turns harrowing, heart breaking, holy and hilarious, these books were like lanterns of truth in an otherwise murky landscape and they made my brain fizz with delight.

So it is with an enormous sense of pride and privilege that we present here for the first time the collected and selected published poetry of Niall Griffiths. Within these pages you will find an unflinching document of a life lived raw, a mind that illuminates the dankest corners of existence and a voice that never ceases to ring anything but clear and bright and true. We have presented the poems more or less as they arrived, a continuous stream of verse scrolling across the pages, one long song of the heart written on the run, dipping in and out of a life lived hard and well if not always wisely.

As someone once remarked, Niall Griffiths is an actual literary star. To that I would add that he's also one of the brightest and most beautiful of souls currently lighting up the pages of this gorgeous fucked up world with awe and rage and wonder.

Long may he burn.
Russ Litten

FOREWORD

The words captured in this book have been harvested from over twenty years' worth of notebooks, fag packets, cereal boxes, post-it notes - any clear and markable surface I could get my hands on, basically. Some of this is indicative of pure pose - look at me, I have so much creativity inside me that I can afford to squander some of it on tatty scraps of paper (forgive me, I was young) - and some of it was pure practical necessity; there truly were times of such chaos and penury that, when the urge to write would strike, there was no clean paper in the room/flat/bedsit whatsoever. I recollect using the white margins of an old newspaper, unrolling the cardboard inner tubes of toilet rolls, anything to create a clean space on which to put down words. One, time, even a kitchen wall . . . I'm making no claims to uniqueness, here; undoubtedly, there are thousands of desperate young men and women across these islands doing exactly the same thing, probably in worse straits than I was then; at least the dole, when I was in my twenties, was seen, if not officially, as the sponsor of the arts; now, of course, it's seen as the stigma of shame, the sign of some profound moral failure.

Well - fuck that. No, fuck *them* and their gleeful, pathetic little cruelties. The young woman in her room, alone, expressing her search for identity and meaning in a flimsy notepad, four for a quid from Poundland - there's more soul and spirit and necessary essence of the terrible human tale in one line of her words than there is in the entire array of neatly-coiffed, sober-suited, shiny-shoed smirking mannequins that hollowly bray from the benches in the House. That's what I gleaned, from going back through all the words contained in this book; it was like an archaeological dig through my own history and psyche, an unearthing of interesting shards, utensils, cave-paintings, all of which proclaim: *Here I was. Look at the life I lived. This is what I saw, and felt, and thought, and listened to, and did.* One person, in his cave, struggling with his addictions, struggling to understand, or at least come to some accommodation with, the internal detonations that always threatened to (and sometimes did) blast him out of the realm of the socially and conventionally acceptable. And the never-ceasing fight for hope . . . Here, in these pages, is the record of such events.

Poetry, though; it's never really been the over-riding, phosphorescent, all-eating need that the novels were, and are - the two urges arise from the same spring, of course, but whereas the novels demand some sustaining sense of futurity, and therefore stability, the poems - or, at least, the kind that I write - are more sudden and galvanic; they leap out of fleeting moments, abrupt instants of joy, sadness, anger, rapture, howling need, intoxication. For the reasons suggested by that, and in deference to the power of such moments, they are printed here pretty much unrevised; regard them as diary entries, as momentous accounts of a lived life - and only a nincompoop would revise their dairies for publication, don't you think? This is why, I suppose, this collection is so varied; I chose (or, rather, was chosen by) the style and typography and rhythm that seemed best suited to each instantaneous emotional event (and to those who might be tempted to carp that some of them are merely chopped-up prose, I would reply: of *course* they are, because if they weren't, they'd just be prose, wouldn't they?). I left out scores, those which didn't work on any level other than to satisfy personal curiosity, and such stuff should never be foisted on anyone else; material of that sort will stay solely and securely on the tatters on which it was written. Maybe in another quarter of a century I'll scoop the cobwebs from my eyes, re-arrange the colostomy bag, hobble over to the shelf on which I store all this stuff and read it all again. And won't that be an experience . . . I might even get a few poems out of it.

Anyway. These blocks of words you're about to read - they are what they are. Like blue whales, like weasels, like the tiny mites that live in your follicles, they just are in the world. I hope at least some of them work for you - to communicate commonality, to offer the relief that is in shared experience. For me, compiling this collection has been an intense, odd, emotionally charged thing to do; I'd open a notebook and see myself as I was at, say, twenty eight, at that wormy, rickety wooden table in the mildewy kitchen, dreading the rap at the door and the brown envelope, scratching at the insects in my skin (both real and imaginary), wondering how I was going to survive the next day, buckling before guilt and need and desperation, flinching from the scratching in the walls, counting the drips come through the ceiling, asking the candle how I'd find the money to re-connect the utilities, and picking up a pen, opening the cheap notebook, putting one to the other and entering a state of vivid, authentic, wondrous and wild alive-ness. How the heart did boom.

ACKNOWLEDGEMENTS

Given that these words span over half the time I've spent on the planet so far, a list of the people from those years who I'd like to thank/kiss/hug/dance with/buy a drink for/watch the moon rise alongside/boot under a train would be twice as long as the book itself, so here's a contemporaneous few who have helped in some way: Russ Litten and family/Andy McPherson and same/Julia Bell/Rebecca Loncraine/Horatio Clare/my uncle Roy/the Humanities Department at Wolverhampton university (in particular Jacqui, Ade, Glyn, Paul Mac, Candi, Dave, Dew - fine people all)/and the one who's stuck it out throughout - Deborah. Also, I'd like to thank all the feral cats that have enriched my life during these years, but they wouldn't give a shite whether I did or not. But I'm going to anyway - them with their mad eyes and claws.

Oh, and I must acknowledge the editors of the many pamphlets and anthologies and chapbooks (most small press, a lot now defunct) in which many of these poems first appeared.

Live well and be happy, despite it all.

NG, Ceredigion, June 2015

CONTENTS

Living In Wales, Aged 26 21
Block 22
11:53 PM (Approx) 22
The Longevity Of Snowflakes 23
As Loaded With Meaning As A Weapon Now Defunct 24
In No Way Like Some Paper Money Stuck To The Sole Of Your Shoe 25
Unspoken Apology.. 26
Spiked 27
Advert Break 27
A Spike From The Star Has Fallen To Earth And Has Gathered
Green Eyes And Fury 28
I Think These Walls Need Painting 29
Jackdaw Dies In Back Yard 30
Disney With A Bazooka And The Tooth Fairy Carries Pliers 31
Needing A Piss 32
Hangover 33
Scene: Niall Having A Shite / Time: 1.38 On A Rainy Tuesday In Aberystwyth /
Soundtrack: "Alison" By Elvis Costello 33
Waiting For The Water To Boil 34
A Morning 35
The Something For Nothing Society.................................... 36
Losing The Moon 36
Sodomy (For K.P.) 37
Mascara 38
A Note On Leaving 38
Justification 39
What If One In Every Thousand Bricks Was Hexagonal? 41
Mountains Grow Like Cancer 43
Nine, Ten, Eleven O'Clock 44
Always Something Dirty About Theory 46
Bedtime.. 46
Seascape, With Gulls 48

For Nobody In Particular	49
Dead Now	50
Tomorrow Is All About Fun	52
Empty Bottle Wednesday	53
My Sadness Once Was Terrible	55
From Me Will Come Flowers	56
October	57
Daylight Saving	58
Blueprint	59
Friendly Fire	60
That's Enough, Now	61
Mourning	63
At Dyfi Junction	64
Another One	66
Winter	67
Beautiful War	68
It's The Ordure Of The Ordinary Which Drives One To Don The Long Coat And Balaclava And Commence Carrying Blades	69
Gravedigging	71
Hope It Snows This Christmas	71
What Shape Is The Sea-Spray In?	72
Because The World's In Colour	73
The Bacteria We Once Were Will Always Breed Within Us	74
Like Love Is Supposed To Be	75
Happy & Happier With Every Drop I Bleed	77
Chain-Smoking Camels	78
How Will I Know When I Get There?	78
Dreams Of Leaving	79
At Thirty-Two	81
When I Write My Masterpiece	83
Listing To One Side But I Can't Tell Which	84
Got To Get This Out; I Can't Concentrate On "A Bit Of Fry And Laurie"	85
Mild Amphetamine Hangover	86
Toxic Psychosis	87

The Beluga	89
Unalone	90
Big Moth In My Kitchen	91
Life Always Finds A Way	91
You, Marry, I, Have, Should	92
One Foot Over The Threshold	92
Portrait Of The Artist As A Young Pisshead	93
Fuck, Yes	94
After Kafka	94
Sometimes, When You Masturbate, Do You Ever Imagine That The Ghost Of A Dead Ancestor Is Watching?	95
At The End Of The Road Is A High Wooden Tower In Which A Man With A Big Gun Stands	96
Insomnia: 1st November, 1993, 7:38 AM	96
Storm	98
Newsnight 1999	99
Getting Wet	101
11:11:99: Total Eclipse	101
Cold Chicken Madras, 9 AM	102
Ten Years On	103
Millennium News	104
In The Doorway Of Barclay's Bank	105
And The Story Of Us All Is An Ongoing One	106
Now I'm Free	106
Driving Around Town	108
Cheap Day Return To The Palace Of Wisdom	109
Nameless	110
My Jesus	111
Rain Is Poison & Sex Is Death	112
Just Like The Blind Man Requires His Guide-Dog; Just Like The Orchids Reach For The Sun	113
To All My Fellow Prisoners	114
Food	114
You're Wishing Your Fucking Life Away, Man	116

Mad Janet Rafferty	119
Bwlch	120
Don't Even Think About It	121
Advice	122
Would You Consider Going Out With An Alien?	123
Just Like I've Always Dreamed	124
If I Heard Her Call My Name	125
A Little Drop Of Moisture On A Packet Of Rizlas & You Lose The Whole Fucking Lot	126
Screaming Blue Murder	127
So The Run-Over Cats Can Prowl Gracefully Into Heaven	128
Flea-Bite	129
With Your Hand Out The Window No-one Can Tell Whether You're Seizing The Day Or Waving Goodbye	129
Truth	132
Visiting Whittington	133
Sally Redwine	135
Lovely Dirty Nasty Brutal Ugly Fucked-Up Gorgeous World	138
Repeats	139
Haiku: Ponytail	140
Hair Of Auburn Water	141
The Luckiest Man In The World	141
After A Glorious Dream Of Fucking Four Women	143
Answering Back	145
Living	146
Scratching	146
My New Boots	147
E#1	149
Sad	150
Sunday Drunk	151
Dead Dog Dreams	152
When You Read This	153
The Genius	154
12/09/1996: Three Oh	156

Drying Out	158
Poor	159
All Of This Only	160
Another Muggy Night	163
Don't Answer The Door, Ignore The Phone	164
Like Some Half-Remembered Nightmare	165
Maybe It's Different In Sweden	166
Diazepam	167
I Think I Need To Get Out More	168
Pasta Bake	169
Rubbing The Lamp	170
When Stars Hum Like Bad Reception	170
Raising Aberystwyth	171
Shock Upon Shock Upon Shock	173
If Fairies Can Be Squeezed From A Bottle	173
Wednesday	175
Storm Warning	175
Dead Dog	177
Colm Recovering	179
Strength	181
For Once	182
Finally	183
God, What A Night	184
Fuck All To Worry About	186
Pus	187
Knowledge	189
Cocaine	189
Finding	190
Free	191
Going To The Pub Where Polly Will Be	193
Susan And The Stairs	194
More Dog Dreams	196
Wrecked	197
Like The Luminous Ghosts Of Bones In An X-Ray	199

Without Fail	199
Rejection Slip	200
Couch	201
One For The Road	203
Pilgrimage	203
Freakshow	204
Why? Well, Listen	205
Ram The Tree Up The Angel's Arse	206
Stoned	208
Everything Is Clean	208
Coitus Interruptus	209
Waving A Can Of Stout Like A Black Flag Of Truce	210
Morning Sunlight, Colour Of Cider	211
Helicopter	212
Visitation	212
After Shaving	213
Mould	215
Suicide Note	216
Liverpool 8, 4 AM	217
Wondering Who I'd Be If I Wasn't Born Me	217
A Dream	219
Liverpool 5, Kosice 0	221
Animals	222
Training Pool For Injured Swans	223
Scabies	225
The Mersey In My Veins	226
Hackles	226
Get In, Get Out, Stop Fucking About	229
Wet Dream At 32	229
No Questions Asked	230
Coming Up To Armistice Day, 1998	232
This Just In	234
Insomnia	235
All Grown Up	237

Open All Hours	239
Three Wishes	241
Smudged	242
Some Reasons	245
Homewards	246
Higher Power	247
Because If You're Already Horizontal, No-One Can Knock You Down	248
Dreamlessly	250
Breaking Through	250
Hillsborough	251
Halloween, 1997	252
Getting Ready To Go Out	254
Necessity	254
Can You Imagine How Hot It Was, To Make That Place Seem Cold?	255
Dishwasher	257
You Don't Always Have To Try It To Know You Won't Like It	257
Never Wear White Boxer Shorts On A Six Day Drinking Binge	259
My Friend Rat	260
Awe	262
Old Man In Search Of Discarded Pornography	263
Gorgeous	263
When It Comes	264
Tariff	264
Cell	265
Surrendering	266
Nevertheless	267
In A Field In Saughall Massie	267
Acceptance	268
Just Feel How My Heart Is Beating	269
Strong Legs	270
Big Brother	271
Pack Up Your Troubles	272
During A Typing Break	273
Red Berries	274

Don't Let Me Fall	275
February 2006	277
A Hood To Hide Your Face	278
Then	279
Don't Cry For Me Cos I'm Going Away	280
The Cobbler's Down The Cobbled Alleyway	281
Poetry	283
Drought	284
A Happy Memory	284
Oh My Goodness, What A Performance, And Just Listen To That Crowd	286
Do This And You'll Feel Better	287
Let Me Go First	287
Drained	288
Spring Morning	290
Type 2 Diabetes	291
A Grief That Hasn't Happened Yet	292
Ex	293
One Question And An Answer	294
Here Endeth	295
Banks Of Fog Like Big White Pillows	295
Bombay Insomnia	297
Don't Mark Me	298
Penrhyncoch Insomnia	299
Temazepam	299
September Afternoon	300
Tuesday Nov 11th: Remembrance Day, 2008: 90 Years After The Armistice	302
It's More Okay Than It's Ever Been, Sometimes, Like Right Now	304
Toothpaste	306
'I Know I'm Odd'	307
Still & Small, Still & Small	308
On The Fourth Or Fifth Day Of Knowing You	310
A Moment To Get My Breath Back	310
As Always, As Rare	312
Robin	313

Indelible	314
'Sometimes I Get Such A Fright'	315
Lust	317
Archeology	318
What We Do With Tongues	318
Giving Up Smoking	319
More Than Half In Stupid Love	321
Almost Imperceptible	323
Two Shades Lighter Than Dijon Mustard	324
A Lesson In Grammar	326
As Close As We May Ever Come	327
Thursday	327
Llanberis Pass	328
April, End Of	330
Recalled	331
A Present	332
Room Service	333
Lines Written After Visiting Tintern Abbey	334
Squawk	335
About Ten Past Three, Maybe	336
White Flag	338
Working Girl	339
Daft Terry Mulligan	341
Hard Sky	342
New House 1	343
New House 2	344
New House 3	345
Simplicity	346
Fame Academy, 2003	346
His Little 'Hello' Noises	347
Okay	348
Ticks	349
Twins	351
I Am Full Of Life	352

A Lot Less Often Now But Still They Come	353
Little Bit Of A Sing-Song	354
Special Delivery	355
That Stupid Club	357
New World	358
Facebook	358
Binge	359
Jarvis Cocker Stole My Audience	361
St Francis Of Assassins	362
We Could Be Outlaws, Just Like We Planned	364
Fortuitousness	365
Young	366
I'll See You When I See You	367
More Shame	368
Four Days And Counting	370
Bad Night	371
Some-Fucking-Thing	372
Not Quite Mushrooms	374
Mouse	375
Regret	376
In A Valley Outside Crickhowell	378
Shared House	379
Chicago	380
A Happening	381

LIVING IN WALES, AGED 26

Some slices of time I think that
it really won't matter if I never see you again;
and, in some others, the anguish of not
touching you threatens to be more than the
whole world can bear. It's neither the
morality or the mortality, it's something
like the lack of filling – which is no simile
but the only way known of outlining the
pain of incompletion. Clear as summer rain
at times; others, murky as the sea slopping
around sewage outlets. Mostly, though, the
clarity is instantly irrelevant, except it
spins out wishes for endless desert escarpment
broken only by skittering lizards and the shadows
of birds soaring in majesty and jagged
hunchbacks of dark rock. And the
invisible breath from heaven of sirocco wind,
land untrod by your beautiful feet but
none the less whole and wanted for that,
land existing firmly, an antidote to the
precariousness always smirking on the edge of
waking. I don't know if you'd care anymore,
but really I think that you would. Like
the thousands of dead starfish washed up
on the beach: I picture your face, your
body's response, your hands reaching to
return them to the sea. Yes, you'd care
if you knew, I know you would. Choir
of seagulls outside; the drone of a washing
machine somewhere in the building. No date,
no time, no signature: This will do.
Did we ever need anything more?

BLOCK

Nauseous it is
I turn my head and India spins

If the writing concerns me
then if I can't write
do I cease to exist

This means nothing

Tonight memories only
nibble
and for that
I thank you,

white block of airy nothingness

11:53 PM (APPROX.)

In the pub tonight they're slaughtering
sheep
hung by their heels from the rafters
pint-glasses agog with blood
scarlet foam

the workers in the abattoir
wordlessly carry placards
my name on each one
in arterial purple

eyes in the hedgerows
each death has an audience of snickers
grass is as calm as eider down
each little murder
each little anguish
each little heart
imploding
there is no moon tonight - give gratitude

THE LONGEVITY OF SNOWFLAKES

Singing as if in a cathedral
        heard from afar
in the bellies of pregnant women
    unlike the rotting dead
      gurgling through country lanes
squeak and gibber
      things fall apart
in the top branches of the tallest trees
      phantoms roost and
aim spit at the heads of passers-by
       a grey essence
formed from genes and surroundings
       and that which greets the infant singing
bringing it all back
      the perfect sphere
which ends in what lies outside:
       the oily blackness of unpitted olives

AS LOADED WITH MEANING AS A WEAPON NOW DEFUNCT

No doctor tells me
I have but a short time to live
because I haven't been to see one
for quite some time

shit bubbles
on four channels
which happen
everywhere

through my door the postman slides
moon rocks pounded paper-thin
by a descending sheet of unbearable pressure

into the pages of daily newspapers
the newsagent slips philosophical
conundrums written by a ballerina
with Down's Syndrome

while in here I carve
faces in the margarine
Lammergeyers out of cheese
and stare at the whirlpools
in the sink
the blizzards
of hair on the diffident walls

To apologise would really not solve anything
least of all the way my mind
hops between stasis sickness sanity and
hysteria
and things as many as squeaks of pain

coffee hovers, an incipient soma
and in code the newsreaders ask me why,
if time is an endless string that can be
reeled in around my wrist, why I
still miss her so hideously much

IN NO WAY LIKE SOME PAPER MONEY STUCK TO THE SOLE OF YOUR SHOE

It's like the first damp cigarette on a hangover
you gag
you heave
but smoke it down to the filter anyway.
Certain eyes and skin and hair and teeth
are the same, are like that;
you know that nearing them
will generate some adverse bodily reaction
such as the gut-fucking
of knowing
that the white horse from the sea-bed
will never
ever
appear
yet the holes still scream to be plugged.
There is no answer; except, maybe,

give up smoking
don't get drunk
go blind.

UNSPOKEN APOLOGY

I have done something
akin to dynamiting
somebody's dear moon,
I have spewed out
convened inhibition,
spat into the eye of a rose,
and for doing so now my
lungs burn with a cold blue flame
and behind my eyes lies
gravel. Sometime soon
I will say I am sorry,
but added to the air we
breathe from hereon in
will be a deep, sharp thing,
dark, dark blue and hung
from the sky between us
like fly-paper, blanket,
shroud. Irretrievable.
Fuck. I am sorry.

SPIKED

It seems   at times
    that this life and all
its little components
      are only the delirium dream of agony

while I somewhere   twitch
mis-happed   slipped
an iron railing in my jaw
         and through my face

in too much pain to
      even allow
          a scream
pissing   whining   and
    waiting to be freed

ADVERT BREAK

Sega computers
a mound of skulls man-high
picked at by birds

Renault
church-bells hang
a flower calyx
booming outbloom of spring and death

Coors beer
somewhere I've never been
America, I mean, not drunken-ness

Twix ice-cream
sand in the toes
and cool on the eyeballs

Kodak disposable cameras
your face I'll look at
until it crumbles to powder

Tampax
beautiful legs
and something I'll never know
in this life anyway

Part 3.

A SPIKE FROM THE STAR HAS FALLEN TO EARTH AND HAS GATHERED GREEN EYES AND FUR

Old and fat
my cat

shaped like a swollen liver

can greenly stare into those parts of me
which only he can enter

carries as much memory between his
bitten ears as I
carry in my lungs

like:
your hand touching
and the sound of your laugh

buoyed by the constant recollection
of seeing his reflection
in a pool of deep ruby blood
hissing and sizzling
on original sand
beneath a blue and
careless sky

I THINK THESE WALLS NEED PAINTING

If I was to return home one night
and find the whole place trashed
I would cook some pasta
open a bottle
sit by the window
among the wreckage
staring at the sea
and pretend that I once had a love
who disappeared one stormy night
several years ago
never to be seen again
and pretend also
that I had a cat
who would approach me carefully
through the junk
green-eyed and murderous
and stare puzzled

at the smile on my face
JACKDAW DIES IN BACK YARD

Masturbating on my bed
in summer storm swelter
and there's a flapping outside the window
in the back yard. Shorts up and
face-wipe I go outside and it's
a jackdaw, can't fly properly,
broken blunder into walls flies
at my face with javelin beak
I duck and he's in through my
bedroom window. Shite.

Some fiend's banner, calling to battle.
An angel's sloughed virtue, squawking to war.

Back inside and he sees me and flaps,
soars across the room and smack
into the bedroom window, dazedly
shakes his head on the sill.
Gently, I guide him out.
He cartwheels into a corner of the yard
and squats there. I break some bread
for him to eat and he ignores it.

Sky suddenly boundaried,
no blue, no cloud, no air.
Yet even here between brick and timber
black wings butcher space like blades.

Later, I go out to see him
and take my washing off the line.
He's cowering in the corner, a
black and breaking thing, beak
gasping, pink tongue twitching,
blue-rimmed eyes obsidian
swivel. Ten minutes later and
he's supine, feet up, curled
claws clasping for the grey
and negligent sky. I put
him in a carrier-bag
and then into my bin.

A nest somewhere, straw and spittle,
eggs among stolen
silver things. A gap now
in the sky. Maybe a mate,
cresting the tree, lookout and
ruffled like an archaic
rare black cap.

DISNEY WITH A BAZOOKA AND THE TOOTH FAIRY CARRIES PLIERS

Elmer Fudd as Cupid
hits a little bird with his arrow
said bird flies to another bird
knocks her out with kisses
builds a house in a tree in
ten seconds flat and carries
her over the threshold in his wings.

It's not that easy, of course.
I mean, look: Daffy Duck
tells Elmer to 'beat it, bub',
which you would do too
before painting a target on your chest
and begging for his bloated arrow to
bruise and blunder all the way
through your fucking useless heart

NEEDING A PISS

Pleasant pressure of internal clasping
juice sluiced and waiting
glans stinging, balls crawling
do this: move to the toilet
stand, feet apart
penis out and held in right hand
between fore-finger and thumb
urinate, piss, micturate
shake off, replace penis
flush toilet, wash and dry hands
(maybe smell them first)
return to seat, cigarette and television.
This lock in my body, lifting
slow thought like a wheezing barge.
The effort of all this.
The horror of its non-appearance.

HANGOVER

As if there were guillotines on the shore
as if ostriches were the town taxis
as if the memory of a face smashed
through the dial of a grandfather clock
still lingers. As if a wish
to have my dick crispy with sex
will be fulfilled after this next mug
of tea; as if the lovers
learning to lie, as if the fledglings
burning to fly will not one day
wilt like these wild wishes
in dim daylight hanging like the
sick and sudden sun peering through
my kitchen window with the florid
blood-flecked face of a butcher and the
seagulls wheel and the weasels squeal
and fuck it I'm going back to bed.

SCENE: NIALL HAVING A SHITE
TIME: 1:38 ON A RAINY TUESDAY IN ABERYSTWYTH
SOUNDTRACK: 'ALISON' BY ELVIS COSTELLO

'My aim is true'
and so is mine, which is good,
else I'd have to scrub the shit
off the toilet seat.

Which would've made you laugh.
The above lines, I mean, not the
actual thing. Rain beats in my yard,
gurgles down the drain.

Grey quiet. Splash, splash, inside
and outside. If I'll ever see you again.
It would be. The expression on your
face, would you still like what you see?

Grunt. Strain. Come down rain.
Hills parrot-coloured through the fine mist.
Your aim is true, too; but the whole land
you can hardly miss. Can you now.

Would you. I'd like to see you anyway
in any way and you in any way and
then anyway in. But it's been a
while. I suppose. Not really.

Whirr. Soft sound of tissue tearing.
Water slightly salt from the nearby sea.
The whitecaps. When we heard the seals
moaning as we walked on the beach at midnight.

Grunt again, strain harder. Pinch
sphincter. My aim is true. You were
very beautiful and I loved you very much.
The shite is ejected, it falls like rain. Release.

WAITING FOR THE WATER TO BOIL

We have only one desire: To live?
No: to live forever, a thought
which stinks like garbage,
which sticks to the ceiling of the skull
and can only be removed by scraping.
Yet things are heating up; fish

will escape into the cool, cruel,
drowning air, and ragworms will
offer themselves up as garters for gulls.
The window, still streaky with rain.
The kettle boiling with a cancerous gurgle,
steam climbing the walls as if
out of a parapet, beading the paint-
work with drops, pearls, torn-out tears,
select splashes of semen. Ah: The
simple synthesis of coffee and milk.

A MORNING

Trundles slow as woodlice
    thought and tea pass each other
in the   runnel of the gullet
scorched by tobacco smoke
    rising   ruffled like mist by
      the hand of God   to stain
the webby ceiling   a spider's moon
dreams turned to crusted mucus
      sex-wishes biologically inevitable
as undeniable as digestion
it   the hand of God
squeezes intestine like a toothpaste tube
      the day ahead tangled like twine
unraveled by the hand
      of the night   begin with
this move   towards the
bathroom

THE SOMETHING FOR NOTHING SOCIETY

As if this isn't difficult
seeking that which keeps
the blood beating and the bowels moving
and the eyes supplied with input
As if this isn't work
continuing to appreciate the birds
when you know that to bury a face
in their feathers would be
to cause panic and smell kerosene
To find some love
in the monotony of poverty
to admire a dark muscle hoisting bone
As if this is easy
As if this is worthless
As if I need a brain stuck in your slime
and this impossible intensity robbed of all colour
or weight
Fuck you all

LOSING THE MOON

Like a million moths making for
the lying light bulb aglow like the
idea of an idea, an electric pear,
metaphor glues like sewage and titles tip away.

Like the moths, gaining one thing means
losing something else; maybe also like them,
each sleep is a taste of the terror and isolation
whistling incessantly over that blue beach.

Unlike anything known is this hunting,
this soaring machine-less at signal fires,
the unanswerable question of whether this yearning
gains or loses the billion glittering brilliants of a wing.

SODOMY (FOR K.P.)

Simian posturing, the
vast welcome of the proffered centre

In no light to speak of, alternating
faces to arseholes, we're playing on each other
like flesh instruments

Tattoo of glans on duodenum
fingertips feathery on prostate
a soft yielding, a wet snap, and then
pink fish wave in an echoless secret cavern

What our life-span resembles;
this sweaty sacrifice, this
grunting collapse with my face
in your skull, each thrust
pumping a musical blast and your
middle finger goading again
each thrust. Seasonal.
Cyclical. Each part a whole,

heirless and sacrificial, something
somehow saintly. I withdraw
and I am, as I somehow expected
to be, clean.

MASCARA

There are idiots
    with pony-tails
giving cocky answers
    in the Florida keys
herons hunting for herring
    on what used to be a beach
& searching for you like always
    I got lost
        like always
Double-barreled names
        flit like gnats
lost too like dogs
        dogs always lose themselves
I'm drunk   I'm drunk
like a glass of cider
    not particularly pleasant
letters run into each other
    looking for themselves
like me   & the gnats   & the dogs

A NOTE ON LEAVING

If it must be me before you -
aeroplane, road, railway,
cancer, overdose, accident,
drowning – then think this
        think this:
that writing this
in the kitchen
us both fresh from the bath

pies rising in the oven
is sometimes, was sometimes
all I ever wanted
& all that I've ever needed
enough to teach me to speak
as a blackbird does.

And if
in a year's time
you should take a book off the shelf
& gasp as one of my hairs
feathers out from its pages
& you want to follow it
down onto the floor then just wait
                    just wait:
we'll see each other again.

All the machinery
of a clanking life
all the cogs will turn
spin we two together
      & we'll see
        we'll see
          we'll see.

JUSTIFICATION

ask me why rubber tyres
always rise again to the surface

ask me why ice-cream
melts in the sun

ask me why trees
can't go shopping

ask me why empty jam jars
are so fucking sad

ask me why the rottenness
grows & spread & stays

ask me why tarmac
yearns for the snow

ask me why magpies
are good at crossword puzzles

ask me why rats
sit at God's right hand

ask me why the people
who control us
care not for our deaths

ask me why
globalism leads to tribalism

ask me why female molluscs
are growing penii

ask me why our lives
drip with oil & slime

ask me why housewives
open tins of corned beef
at four in the morning
in suburban kitchens

ask me why worlds die

ask me why loss survives itself

ask me why it never comes back

you'll always get
the
same answer,
and that's
probably wrong

WHAT IF ONE IN EVERY THOUSAND BRICKS WAS HEXAGONAL?

Oh yeah, yeah, that
meeting in the bar & you just get on
so fucking well with each other
so much in common
so at ease in each other's company
oh there were silences, aye, but they
were comfortable ones,
& each drink brought more pleasure
& then you went dancing
& there were tiny movements so
unusual, so unique, so redolent
in their miraculous fluid,

and you thought God, God,
I feel like a skier at the top of the mountain,
a goalkeeper at the Bernabeu,
a diver hanging over a mile-deep trench,
& then of course
the sex was fucking magnificent
(how could it be otherwise?)
& waking up together
simply extended the dream,
then the brief times apart
became gorgeous with waiting
& briefer
& briefer
until you weren't apart anymore
& then
& then...

well...

how these things turn out: in
dullness & tedium, over-familiarity,
petty betrayals, timid compromises,
slippered acceptance & apathy
uglier than a maimed animal on a
wheel.

Ah, some things last, I suppose;
a certain way of laughing, maybe,
some generosity with money
or emotion...
a casual touch in the darkness...

but mostly it stays the same;
habitat becomes habitual

with dismaying speed & facility.

Always.

Our homes are not chosen; they are to
do with what is available
& what is necessary.
Why then does it always end this way?
Once, someone told me that
it's not cement & mortar
which keep a wall upright,
it's balance.
You can build a wall, he said,
simply with bricks & sand & water.

Which may be true, I suppose, but
that's all you can do; build
another fucking wall.

Jesus how this
goes on.

MOUNTAINS GROW LIKE CANCER

From ferns through festering fleece
to sky-borne clouds of greasy smoke;
all is web-footed stab & stun,
all is infection & maul.

Turning like turtles waves hiss like doused stars;
rain-clappers toll in natural tents.
Heart-anchored witnessing offers no solace.
Eyes are rooted in hair-clogged drains.

Still, I'll tell you what really pisses me off;
when you drive your shovel into a pile of rubble
& it hits some huge block & immediately stops dead -
all that wasted energy.
I really fucking hate that.

NINE, TEN, ELEVEN O'CLOCK

prowling and
        peeping in people's windows

see them demolish chickens
grease drooling down their chins

drinking tea in the flickering grey
of a television

coal-look fires and
        low lighting
cats and dogs and children

like an x-ray
viewing, violating

what should never be seen
this safety
so simple to smash

see them kiss
torture each other

hand each other sweeties
in the
warmth

caress babies
wear dressing-gowns
fresh from the shower

can almost smell them
they'd smell like
shadowy bushes
after a rain

in summer nights
some windows stay open

thin curtains
bellying, billowing
in the rare breeze

so easy it would be
so
easy

sometimes they hurt each other
might one day witness
a murder

anything
anything to break this
boredom

ALWAYS SOMETHING DIRTY ABOUT THEORY

To assuage, satisfy, or
merely just explain an
ever-present ache we
invent such lies as
can be scratched onto paper
with ink. No-one sees
us in our dirty kitchens
late into summer Sunday
afternoons.
Yet still it seems to gleam; the
hunched back, the scribbling wrist,
the fixed and determined eyes with things
dancing in them, certain, sure, and
if only for this one moment
happy to be here, on this planet,
like an animal eating or
a child at play.

BEDTIME

Honestly, no joke, I can hear an owl
outside hooting in the trees,
remarking on the fact that
the night eats colour,
and the unexplored landscape
recedes into a fluffy blackness,
it's foreground wrestling forests
and a fuzz of bushes
and a river, each ripple of which
conveys every instant

some new beauty or horror
or instant of indifference...

no stars visible in this flat of course,
these walls and floor and ceiling
built for my warmth and comfort
when? I don't know,
but there is gentle salt
beneath my eyelids
and muscles needing replenishment
and many events, none really
extraordinary but events nonetheless,
to be thought through
and assessed
and analysed
in startling and colourful allegory,
as there is always and again
a whole new day
to be prepared for, to be faced,
ah recuperation, preparation,
re-fuelling...
new energies plucked from the dark.

The toilet's faulty cistern
heaves and hisses like a beast asleep.
Midnight. Sober, and content.
Tonight will be a peaceful one: I'm
written.

SEASCAPE, WITH GULLS

Squabbling for scraps in the foreground,
this battle for nourishment
amid winged flurry
and beak-stab,
the background
blue shading to silvery sea
beneath which
we all know
dragons still lurk and shift slowly
like scaly mountains,
all gently washed
by the intense light
illumine
spilling through the cold-cracked cloud,
all this encircled by ---------------

No; wait; what's all this shit?
Why must the landscape be
a psychic one?
The birds, the water,
the sky, all the falling light,
these all exist
independently,
outside utterly
of all us feeble seers,
trembling on the land's edge
in our frantic, grubby searches
for validation, justification,
and power...

It's fucking pathetic. Christ, be
alive, human, be strong;
these lungs that wheeze,
the eye that sees,
the hand that picks and writes.
This is enough.
Learn.

FOR NOBODY IN PARTICULAR

with your head
severed by shrapnel
    in a field of blooming roses
you would look like
    nothing else but a vase

behind the wheel of a car
    you can be, and often are
demonic – pumping petrol
you are every grinning burden
    on this planet's resources

smoking
    you are no garbo
handling money
    you are no getty

I don't know who you are
but I can hear the crash and grind
    of gears in your ears
your breath explodes
    like artillery

you have eyes
and you have hands
and legs and feet
and ears again
but with your head gone
sitting staring stinking
alone in a ditch
several yards away
with your old head
severed by shrapnel
in a field of swaying roses
you'd look like nothing
else but a vase

DEAD NOW

it must be like this
for a dugong foetus
    the slight salty smell
    the biscuit baked light
    the rise and fall of breath and blood
    and the warmth, the warmth
    the dromedary hump of her slumber
and although this is lovely
the squeezing out into light and no-longing
and movement free and fluid
is far lovelier still

in an underground bar
in the hills in Wales
I was first informed; no Kennedy, you,
I'll probably forget that location in time

but then I drank more and drank more
while outside in the rain of stars
falling, falling like a dream of spider eyes
a grass-snake and a badger
    faced each other silently
under a wet and wilting Douglas fir

the clothes and boots which I trip over
the scattered mounds of biscuits
        going mouldy and soft
letters from and photographs of
        things which I'm tempted to
but don't want to see
waiting for the crash, for the shock of
    brock biting

goodbye then, goodbye all the things that
    you ever made count
goodbye all the things you enlivened
you really were a help at times
and I'll never meet you now goodbye
goodbye to the robin I saved
goodbye to the girl with the shaven head
goodbye to the Chinese girl who smelled sweet
        and sour
goodbye to all the things I'll never do
to the girl who now sleeps and waits to grin
goodbye goodbye to the dolphin I dream
about goodbye

why pretend? The soft click on the
multi-coloured triangle, the random
reverberations, the scattering of colour
towards and away towards and away

I'll raise a bottle to it all next time
I get a chance to the light in the
wine imprisoned prismatic the colours running
jumping singing spinning to face then
        suddenly stop

TOMORROW IS ALL ABOUT FUN

at no specific time
did they spread their dark wings
come out of the walls
and circle

I cannot pinpoint the exact time
when they outlined their proposal
their black plan and said
here is addiction
here is alcoholism
this is you promiscuous
drunk
asleep in your own puke
courting violent demise

all this
we will keep you from
if you write
our influence
our chuckling sabotage
the shrapnel of our destruction

let these
be your theme

all of this
they said

and I had no choice
but to agree
and still tomorrow
will glitter and be brilliant

freedom sings
the world cracks open
and will release
a cloud of green parakeets

and I will fly and I will chatter
with them
roost on Everest
eat gold
taste a bit of creation's colossal promise
before I am required to

pick up a pen
again

EMPTY BOTTLE WEDNESDAY

and they are clustered in the bin
greenly gleaming
among the boxes   wrappers   and tea-bags
and peelings, their open mouths
sucking at the ceiling   hungry
like the Asian family
in the Jobcentre

as I sign on, the children crying, the
sea rolls in   rolls in with
the pattern of my hangover

out-of-date milk souring the tea
a police car cruises slowly by
looking for what at 9:45 AM
on a Wednesday, what, Monday
and Tuesday
now dead and buried beneath vomit
and good books that I can't afford

dreams of demonic bed-dwelling
dwarves still stink and linger
but
none of this is unbearable, none of
this
is too much to accept, I am a thief
and a liar and a drunkard   I am
lonely and bitter and
the slime of wine in the throat
will ooze away, ooze all away, everything
will slide down my back
like polluted lake-water
off wing-feathers and I will wear it
like a cape then unwrap myself and
toss it over the back of a chair, just
like this
ash and the postman brings
only a catalogue
of

MY SADNESS ONCE WAS TERRIBLE

here
old people
smartly dressed
wander the lanes
towards the small grey chapels in the trees

& I sat
in a graveyard
on a beach
on the westward edge of Europe
& the wind hit me &
took me

& Times Square
painted my face
the broken blood vessels
& I once wore a cloud like a hat

& little lives lived, lost
in dank burrows
& the escape of birds

& having that thing that follows you
& the isolation from everyone
& the terror in your knees
& the breaking in your throat

the shadows of trees between your shoulder-blades
birdsong buried in the wind

one I lay on my belly
on a beach
& stared at the sand
& thought: if each of these grains
could be me
then why does the sky stay blue?

FROM ME WILL COME FLOWERS

Crackling light in forest-floor mulch.
It feeds the millipede.
Hungry beaks of birds in the branches
stuffed with insects
for their screaming young.
It can come
on a car journey, in summer, driving
back from Liverpool,
in a heated world of green,
the lambs and the pheasants
and the swifts and the swallows
slicing the sky, that
nothing this beautiful can ever be bad.
The bark in the blood.
The phloem in the skin.
Your own face in the arrangement of
chestnut leaves
and it is wearing a smile.
You'll come again, you think -
you've been here before.
On a car journey across green Wales
on a day that bakes
and the universe expands
in your cells,

that oak has its roots
in your feet.
I feel suns in my nucleus,
clouds in my eyes,
I am part of this, all of it,
and death is just part of the deal.
These mountains plan poems fore
future events,
certain future events:
my marrowbone
no pain.

OCTOBER

They're saying that such a good summer
must be followed by a bad winter
and already the white bombs of frost
have blown the toadstools from the soil

and people lean into the wind.
Once, I remember having a dog
and both of us on a shore of ice
leaned together into the cold distances.

But an organ swelled inside him
too big for him to bear and he died.
People talk of the necessity of movement
and all the comforts of going one place

but cold walls prevent you.
You press your nose to the cold, cold glass
and squint through the slanting rain
at the promise of white flowers

and wait for it all to
float into your back yard
but you can't stop telling yourself
that this wait is in vain,
that everything will prove itself
without meaning completely, or hope.

DAYLIGHT SAVING

those white and buckled stalks
in pots of mud in the yard
recently
were flowers

deep night
at 5PM
as the kitchen fills with steam
and the central heating clicks on
and releases the stink
of burning dust
into the flat becoming
dry becoming
airless

and the rain and gales
beyond the glass
don't make it any better

soon now
winter-ribbed foxes
will overturn bins
burst bags and strew rubbish

and kites
will cast their hungry shadows
over the housing estates

spiders will seek the bathroom steam
so to incubate their eggs
as if they know
the purpose of this
as
hanging there only bloated
those stupid sucking sacks of hunger
in knowledge
that this dark time
designed so that Great War farmers
would have prolonged light to work by

remains threatening, unwelcome
and still whispers about death

BLUEPRINT

say you knew nothing of this
& then they gave you a plan -
a map of a human life
with all its days
designed – you would gasp
you would reel
likely you would weep
you would be without
the tiniest shred
of acceptance
or belief
& yet you travel through it

from the students above
playing crap guitar at 4AM
to the girl with the scarred wrists
paying for her milk
& paper

kestrel above the hill
hear this
rain on the sea
smell this

clanking radiator
warm all this
electric lights
illuminate this

& blank black cat at the wet windowpane
mewling for warmth & comfort
help this
help this

FRIENDLY FIRE

And I know that you are desolate now; that,
with the world whirling by beyond
glass, you feel that any
impact at this moment
would be irrelevant, otiose,
some supreme indifference.
But the world is whirling, yes, the
snow shifts under your feet, yes,
and the big birds clatter and cast

shadows in the branches. There
is a cottage for you, somewhere
by a church, and a riverside
walk to the pub and a castle
on the hill that overlooks
the village. You yearn for
too much now in your time
of great falling, this spread
desolation, but the shattered
glass of your soul gives back
the clouds to the clouds. Sand
and locusts and cucumbers
pick at each other inside you.

It is a time for you of frantic damage.
But somewhere there is a church
and a cottage in the shadow
of its Norman tower and
above that, a castle, and above that,
the sky.

THAT'S ENOUGH, NOW

there are vague and faceless figures
drifting at the edge of my vision

and my vision is blurred
has always been
blurred

they drift noiselessly
through nights starless

with longing
with sleep smashed
by footsteps

through dreams of mountains
and lakes

I feel my body decay
I feel my soul struggle

there is an urge
to stand in castles
or on seashores

there is a desperate
birdwish
waveneed

all is silent
even the noise
and it is lonely
as a mountaintop
in mist

all that I've done
all that I am
running like urine
down my trembling leg

there is a loneliness
too vast for the words
of a lifetime

there is a needing
bigger than the stars

love in rubble
sunk in mud

this silence
these drifting shapes

one of you
come before me, into the light

it's time now
for my needle

MOURNING

You've seen millions of them, haven't you?
Or thousands, at least, maybe
tens of thousands – bees & cats
& dogs & clouds & trees & butterflies
& flowers & sheep & cattle
& leaves & blades of grass.
Other things.
Tens of thousands, at least.

Yet there's one, sometimes, that
allures your eye for longer
than usual; maybe it's the light,
the mood you're in, but
there's something about that robin,
in the Y of the branch, about

that cat, asleep on the lean-to roof,
about that pine-cone, a
grenade against the blue.

You look longer.
You gaze. You
study.

Well, energy must be transferred;
carbon is only ever re-arranged.
That floating dandelion seed, flaxen &
white & electric – I saw it last
on my grandmother's head.
And the stain on the moth's wing,
the maroon stain, it's
exactly the same shade
as the blood caught beneath
my granddad's fingernail
from where the anvil caught his hand
in a factory. Ten
thousand times
you've seen these things, ten
thousand times at least.

AT DYFI JUNCTION

There is just me & the wind
& the chittering chirruping birds &
a newspaper.

I remember Mr. Gilmour
teaching Edward Thomas's 'Adlestrop' &
talking about calmness & caesura, necessary,

& reflection, & age, & childhood.
Gilmour wasn't unbearable.

I could've changed trains at Machynlleth
& spent an hour there
with the cafe & shops
but Dyfi Junction has an osprey
& nothing else
but wind & birds
& distant mountains
& an isolation.

I put my newspaper into the bin
& smoke & piss off the platform
onto the sleepers & gravel.
Birds sing. It is a bright & sunny
day. The train to the northern coast
is not due for some time,
time enough to read
& smoke
& sit & stare
& stroll up down the platform
& hear the birds & the sheep
& the cows & the wind
in the trees & the rushes.
White cottages dot the distant hills.
Nearby trees are stunted & bent by a wind
that can blow as merciless as birth
& I am alone & happy, filled with
a multitude
in a place unpeopled
& I hear, again, Gilmour's voice,
faint & at a tremendous distance,
& there's only one me in the galaxy.

In the wind in the grasses
& the musical birds
you may speak to me too; I am your
servant & I have ears
to heed your voice. But
know this: if you set me aflame
& fill me with fire
there will be a time
when all I am is ashes.

ANOTHER ONE

I contain things that are
far far bigger
than what I am that
miniaturise
that which holds them

& when you clamped your hand over my mouth
& your other hand clutched my nape
so that I wouldn't make a noise
so that I wouldn't cry out
& for a second I saw your eyes
before I closed mine

then I knew that here was another one
another universe
another infinity
inside this wrecked & shaking
little body

WINTER

Lacewing views oblivion
in the dew-planeted threads
of Charlotte's house
the waves wish to be iced
the shores wish to be warm
the longest local road is a frozen Styx
and the raven thinks he's Charon
carrying black the carrion-bird
cackles a claxon
for the silent maelstrom of emergencies
craneflies waltz in cathedrals of frost
sharpening the transient
infinities of mucus
in winter
the postman delivers gulls
disemboweled on the thorns of slow trauma
in winter
the policemen place live coals in their boots
which throb like the eyes of a baby
cold and cribbed and quaking
in a chemist's dripping doorway
in winter
the cows gather in grey hollows
to tell tales of terror
their dreams of bolt-guns
conveyor-belts, the smiling of knives
and the rumble of exhaust
in winter
things kill
other things
this winter gives

BEAUTIFUL WAR

Surroundings do inform the sentences
so black-and-white TV and
dirty dishes and a smelly ashtray
all encapsulate those times
we wrestled in utter comfort
and fought bloodlessly with
big gulping grins and of
course the times we bloodily
fought with fangs that gnashed
and words that went wham but
then to re-group on the bank
of the bed hot in the flames
of the expensive gas fire and
several other things which burned
like the sparks everywhere
which spat like snakes and the
feel of your fingers across my
skin going all yodelly and the unfound
shapes your limbs would form
most definitely unlike the
shell-shattered letters of soldiers
and your face and hips at the window
welcoming me through the gravestones
and your voice my God your voice
would be the mortar in the walls
of the house we shared and will
tin in my ears for as long as
I remember the baby bird which
died and the sinews on the backs
of your knees and the tiny scar
between your breasts like a

comma oh sand-dunes I
think of the times we were so
easily able to ensure that things
stayed behind the glass such
as the snow we kicked through
that rainy Christmas the
lights from the shops spun sun
on your already golden face and
Christ how I hold this with
me through all my faulty
dealings in which some kind
of rotten-ness deepens and threatens
to spread like it always will
I know I know not a cell
not an atom of what you
are moving through now
but forever I will carry
the scars the prompting marks
little lovely legacies of a
beautiful war in which
we never ever called a truce

IT'S THE ORDURE OF THE ORDINARY WHICH DRIVES ONE TO DON THE LONG COAT AND BALACLAVA AND COMMENCE CARRYING BLADES

Rent
in the armour of a whale
leaks shrieking as if the planet is raped
the earth torn with the screech of mauled
                                              metal

through pours darkness as black as an
anorexic's excrement
and mine is in arrears; I'll lose my flat if I
don't clear them up soon.

Gas
hangs on every limb like a hand-me-down
falsely promises some pretty thing
has the smell of danger, of a cankered
                              balance
neatly between this pit, that platform
and will be cut off if I don't pay the next
installment on my Budget Payment Plan.

Fees
are a pre-requisite
afterbirth wobbles like a moneyed man
why these sleeping bags of pine? For
reassurance, when we could feed the fish
and the dogs
but I'll be removed from college if I don't
soon pay what I owe.

Bill
those words this pen these thoughts
peck at chickenweed at offered bread
suckle ducklings or crunch their bones
lift laces of leeches from the garbage
I have a slate to clear at the shop
but that's OK because the owner is kind
but there's guilt to be cleared too.
Whetstone. Wool. Steel. Crombie.

GRAVEDIGGING

Some people can live their whole lives
loving, or at least believing they do,
a god, or a celebrity, or an ideal,
without ever seeing their faces

and I suppose I can too, although
I wouldn't know which category of idol
to put you in. can. I can.
But if could, I'd prefer not to
see your face anymore, in this way:
there it is in the clouds again.
The shapes of suds in the bathwater.
In the smile of a happy cat.
Somewhere it still exists,
brownly, widely smiling,
eyes as big and green as this earth
across which immense, terrible and
beautiful lizards once walked.

HOPE IT SNOWS THIS CHRISTMAS

And, oh, another:
    it's night-time
and we are standing at the guard-rail
    of a ship looking out at the moon
and a vast and endless ocean
    we're holding hands
and widely smiling
    you're wearing a long and battered overcoat

and all your hair is in your face
>   but I can still see your eyes

flying-fish soar below us

you hold your hair out of your face
and move silently towards me
as the first person steps to the rail
ties a brick around his neck
prays to the stars and leaps overboard

WHAT SHAPE IS THE SEA-SPRAY IN?

& yet another, Christ, they won't leave me
alone tonight;
>   a sunny afternoon
& we stand in the ruins of an ancient abbey
>   in an ancient northern city
eating ice-creams with sticky hands
>   smelling the green river behind the trees
wondering at the peacocks
>   the great fans of colourful eyes
I watch you watching them
>   & anticipate how, later,
when I take your clothes off,
>   my heart will beat like the sound of
artillery fire. I say something
>   & you laugh – or perhaps it was the
other way round - & we finish the ice-
creams & go home. But
this one really happened.

BECAUSE THE WORLD'S IN COLOUR

You're puzzled
at what seems to be coming apart,
why it's happening just when
you thought you were cemented;
your anger
your yearning
your idiot exile
the cloud
which hovers between you and the presence
which will not break its silence
the fog
in your hungover brain
starved of oxygen, moisture,
withered with salt
an old and sprouted potato
at the bottom of the fridge.
Summer has gone
and the rains have come.
You stand by your open window
and reflect
on the fact
that those fuzzy grey figures
on the reels of wars One and Two
are now all dead; if not
by bomb or bullet
then merely by mornings, afternoons,
evenings. Just hours
of lightlessness.

THE BACTERIA WE ONCE WERE WILL ALWAYS BREED WITHIN US

You think
that they might never come again
& here's
a night you get three.

Maybe just
as distractions
from your loneliness
but nevertheless – here's
a night
you get three.

You're clean,
well-fed,
healthy.
Money is on its way
& tomorrow you'll be
whole again.
Inspiration, motivation -
they're no problem.

& now
just when you thought
they might never
come again,
here's
a night you get three.

Why then
does it feel like
your
heart is breaking?

Into many little
pieces?

LIKE LOVE IS SUPPOSED TO BE

You think you've built up an armour
you think that now you're protected

you avoid
what you must avoid
& seek
what you must seek

but it ambushes you
from the most unlikely corner:
like when
you're looking up satay recipes
on the web
& you find a menu for a Chinese restaurant
in Robertsbridge
so you look up Robertsbridge
while on the TV
orcas
swim & blow
through a lagoon
pine forest behind them
snow-capped peaks

& Robertsbridge
is down south somewhere
a place you've never been
&
it's there, in you,
the hollowness
the longing
this strange & soaring yearning
& you take a shower
on the radio
a song says 'gravity, you are my enemy'
& you cook pasta
& write in front of some banal programme
voices in your ear

so you don't start weeping
so you don't think of dying
so you don't think of heartbreak

because
it never leaves
it waits for you
the black destroyer
the reeking thing

telling you of loss
& pain
& a dissatisfaction so deep

one with the owls you'll never be
with the orcas you'll never be
& this attendant thing

will be a shadow among the mourners
the veils & the suits
in the rain
at your grave

HAPPY & HAPPIER WITH EVERY DROP I BLEED

& you begin to re-inflate
like a recently squeezed sponge
        suds on the sheets
trails of nails
vampiric snails
blood & sweat & come & spit
the curtains bellying
        squelch
& pop
pant
& relax winding down so slowly
        so quickly
this room & us
we clench & glue
feet drag across sodden sheets
it hurts a bit
& I cannot squeeze you hard enough
bird sing & a car rumbles
I am so happy
so fucking happy
my blood is smeared across your face
& I have not been
    this happy
    for a long
        long time

CHAIN-SMOKING CAMELS

It's OK; it's more; it's good,
no money but we're really alright,
the car's on the road again &
summer's sliding softly in,
my body is hardening
& my brain is slicing off of itself
the edges ripped & ragged by recent rages,
hot water in the tank again
& the rent is paid in advance; I
couldn't, at this moment, with
any justification, really ask for more;

yet even now I know that later,
in the bath, the water will turn foggy red.

This is no time to feel robed
in the blood of Jesus.

HOW WILL I KNOW WHEN I GET THERE?

There are times when
I catch a glimpse of
myself
unexpectedly,
say in a mirror behind a bar,
white face split in a grin
eyes burst in dark fire

or in a shop window
as I move past
in a natural slouch
shoulders set to swing
slight unhappy snarl

      I see my face
      in
      cracked mirrors
       tiled floors
        buckled chrome

looming
over a mirror
striped with speed
moneysnorkel in the nostril
incomprehensible volcanoes
in the skull

& I think:
yes. I'm still here

DREAMS OF LEAVING

Bringing the washing in out of the rain,
Sunday papers crinkling the couch,
fridge humming, coffee on the boil,
the latest one asleep in the bed...

all of this – is
this all there is?

This happens sometimes,
but always regular -
all of this was burped out one evening
by a sick seagull
fed too many chips
by holiday-makers,
& this all becomes
something to run away from,
like quicksand
or fire
or illness,
not that mixture
of enticement & allure
& repetition & fear
like hard drugs or
sex with someone wild-eyed
or a tiger, say; no, this is
not like that at all.

This all stays here
this goes on
while my head seethes
with Peru, County Mayo,
the Outer Hebrides...

there's not much else to say.
These dreams of leaving never leave.

AT THIRTY-TWO

You
spend a lot of time on your own.
Some of it is necessary,
for the writing,
but sometimes
you get lonely.

You have a god-daughter,
who is beautiful,
but no children
of your own.

You love your girlfriend
and spend a lot of time
talking to her
on the telephone.

You
smoke too much
and
when you have the money
drink a great deal.
That
nameless sense of loss and terror
and doom
that stole your sleep as a child
still afflicts
you
on occasion,
although you think maybe
that you're learning to cope with it.

You think a lot
about
a dog and a cat who both died of tumours
fairly recently.
You dream about them, sometimes,
and you miss them both
terribly.

You
love your family.

You hate Manchester United
and the braying middle-class cunts
who support them
passionately, on both counts.

You are deeply aware
of how the presence of birds
enriches
your life.

You masturbate
when hungover
then feel
dirty and polluted.

You like
the taste of chocolate,
and the smell of honeysuckle
and coffee.

There is nothing,
you think,
that could improve your life,

except for more money; you
are poor and you dislike it.

You think a lot
about your coming
death – when it will happen,
and in what
manner.

WHEN I WRITE MY MASTERPIECE

The balustrades will sing
accompaniment to the lungs collapsing
   bags emptied of their groceries
a celebration of loss, of the end of joy
   small, beautifully coloured caged birds
singing so sweetly for their blinded eyes
the sky yanked away like sabotage

Then, surely, there will be reason to do it
to appease the accessible angel
dragging this digging, pushing this pen
casting eyes on every movement
   every grasp, every reaching
late-night screenings of the most
   vile movies imaginable
for this audience of one

There'll be no hesitation when it happens
when I write my masterpiece
there'll be nothing to
   keep me breathing

      only soil   rich, moist and smelling of life
      only nothing   singing with the voice of the
                          last fin whale
only the memory of you
     in your giant perfection
       with all its flaws

I'll do it, I promise
I promise, I'll do it
    the overdose at dawn
    with all the birds singing
    fly away fly away
    I will I'll do it
when I write my masterpiece
when I cease to remember you

LISTING TO ONE SIDE BUT I CAN'T TELL WHICH

These things:
some tobacco, papers and a Zippo lighter
Marlboro reds
Garfield cup smelling of coffee
crumbs on a plate
blue flower border
this pen this page
Django's shattered hands.
Chin in need of a shave.
A bad taste on the tongue.

More? Yes, yes, of course;
invisible boxes tied to my back
like cans on the bumper of a marriage hearse

see how they tumble
watch them roll
filled with things which when rattled
make a noise like breaking bones

GOT TO GET THIS OUT; I CAN'T CONCENTRATE ON "A BIT OF FRY AND LAURIE"

two children
a boy and a girl
both little
playing on a beach
found a packet labeled
'INSTANT SEA MONSTER: Just Add Water',
with a picture of a bright green
toothlessly smiling
serpent
and a list of ingredients.
They looked at each other
laughed
opened the packet
and poured it, the powder,
into the sea.

And were found,
later,
in several jagged
pieces
on the sand
ripped open
their entrails
wrenched out

eyeless
toothless
hands that would be clawing
if they weren't fingerless
impossible to tell
which was boy
which was girl
their intestines
still steaming
spelling out, on
the crushed, hot rock
these words:
PLSOWX
and
ZRUAVB.

MILD AMPHETAMINE HANGOVER

When I'm in the bath under suds
   steam rises   relaxed hands move upwards
then I know, with utter conviction,
how this jaw sore with forgotten babbling
and remembered bruxism
and thigh muscles aching with impurities
and unshakeable sensations of sadness
are one, are all one big One,
with wisdom in whisky and the
gentle perennial dizziness of this world's turning.

And I'm thinking of my friends
alone in their beds
   curled   threatened   and waiting for sleep.

Linger on, all of you.
Twenty-seven approaches
and the trees weep for the children
for all of the children.

It's only after the rush that
realisation of the need's reasons
hits. My family, I think of;
broken birds in the gutter; the
night when you went and how I
didn't think of how I'd remember
so clearly your face in the sodium
for the rest of my life.

Food is no sustenance.
The rain drips
wind whines.
I'm thinking of the people who affect this life
and how I love to think of them.

TOXIC PSYCHOSIS

If you look askance
out of the blood-laced corner
of your bald and bursting jittering eye
you'll notice that all the random people
possess horse's heads
or their own heads worn backwards
and they know when you're about to
stare at them levelly
and then they put on normal heads
some of them prettier

and avert your war-fraught eyes
behind which frisk
sharp metallic objects
roaring iron dinosaurs
terror of exposure
the craving to kill whoever
has power in any form over you.
Each morning arrives with the aroma
and sound of avalanche
each night with the grunt
of a sated beast
hauling itself out of bloodied swamp.
The only concentration
can be in the frantic kaleidoscope
swarming like stinging insects
in your wet and flapping lips
limbs replaced when you weren't mentally there
now alienly flop
seeking to return to their rightful owner
now slumped and truncated
and gagged in a bed somewhere.
Food would hit you like a mainline of spew
and bed would only be a harbour
for some bristling stinking thing
crawling up your legs.
There can be no ending to this.
The world can be sniffed up your nose.

THE BELUGA

Is here again
this time he's been away for quite a while
but he's back now, most definitely back
a little more polluted
a little more scarred
but still as white as the moon
with a smile which had been waiting for
millions of years before my birth
knowing that sometime I would appear.

The beluga
is here again
the canary of the sea
his organs seethe with additives
but his whole being rings with song
I welcome him completely
but still sometimes attempt to
push him gently into the background
but he's too big, too strong
and too beautiful
for me to put any real force into my hand.

The beluga
is here again
circling my head, amusedly studying
as I write this, make coffee
wait for sleep, ablute
weaving between my legs
riding me on his island back
how can I ignore him?
He knows I can't

and that's why he continues to return
and that's why, despite everything else
he's never able to be sad.

Beluga
you are here again
you have taught me once more to sing
and although your visits are always
only temporary
nevertheless at each one
I rejoice, and even when
you are not here
I know you are visiting somewhere else
and when I hear you begin to sing
very softly and far away
I know you are coming back.

UNALONE

Because
that fucker is back again
standing behind me
grinning
unshaven
halitosis
a machete in his grubby fat paw.
I hate him. I fucking hate him.
He has a moustache
and a hideous white beer belly
and he stinks, he really fucking stinks,
of all things sad and hurting and lost.
This time, he says, this time

he'll be around for quite a while.
He's in no rush.
He's fat and he's heavy and I can't shift him,
I simply can't.
There is no hope.

BIG MOTH IN MY KITCHEN

Sticks to the wall, a shadowed heart
wingbeats the whisper of a phantom
beautiful insect seeking the moon
beautiful insect sheltering from the rain

LIFE ALWAYS FINDS A WAY

Some morning soon
you will wake up
throw off the blankets
stumble yawning to the window
slide open the curtains
&
see below you
a Guinness-head layer of ruffled cloud
lit from beneath
with a lovely, pulsing, lilac light
& for once
you will not feel the urge
to climb back into bed

YOU, MARRY, I, HAVE, SHOULD

The only ring of yours I ever wore
was your sphincter muscle
clinging golden and perfect
on my middle finger
whilst lip to lip
I played on your body
like an ancient instrument
used to enchant the sun.

I know it wouldn't have worked,
but this is worth it,
this hurting yearning, the thought of you old and still in my life,
dressed in mourning,
so beautiful in black you looked,
head bowed and veiled at the lip of my grave
with your eyelashes jeweled with rain.

ONE FOOT OVER THE THRESHOLD

& my heart was beating so fucking fast it could
be seen through my shirt like something
a polecat perhaps attempting to escape & the
blood was a frenzy in my fingers and my knees
were unset cement and my eyes burned as
they looked there & there & oh my God there
& synapses fizzed as they strove to commit the
sights to memory how golden it was how
golden how gorgeous there was a boundless
sea of another self to plunge in & oh so
many new things to discover so new so

wondrous so full of unseen colour & lungs
rasping with the acceptance of future feverish
heartbreak I knew it was there but I didn't
care the world asked me was it worth it &
Jesus Christ with his agony & his view of
those faces thump thump thump thump yes
it was of course it was oh yes of course oh fucking
yes oh yes oh yes my God fucking yes

PORTRAIT OF THE ARTIST
AS A YOUNG PISSHEAD

& ah shit – I've done it again,
potatoes roasting in the oven,
madmen on the television,
the worst hangovers are those blurred ones
where you have some hairy memory of
an unspeakable thing
& you shake your head
over morning tea &
your skull and baggy face move
but your brain stays static
& it can simply not get through
that the red-eyed rats
& the high-stepping deer, fawn in the dawn,
love this wonderful life but all the same
       if they had a choice
would sometimes maybe prefer
       not to live it

FUCK, YES

Notoriously elusive, is God;
      we have sought him
        in landscapes
          waves
          planets
the eyes of beautiful animals
      in intricate thought processes
but for 5 billion years he
has remained invisible
indeed
at times he has seemed to insist
on his non-existence   yet
when he steered us towards each other
that breezy night between brine
the whole universe heard him
      roaring   roaring
in triumph   with laughter
ecstatic for once with his creation

AFTER KAFKA

Imagine if you were dragged out of bed
                        at dawn
to face twelve armed policemen
                        who then
read out a long list of charges
                so vile
                so hideous
                so utterly
                evil

that they remained in your head
$\qquad\qquad\qquad$ for
$\qquad\qquad\qquad$ ever

SOMETIMES, WHEN YOU MASTURBATE, DO YOU EVER IMAGINE THAT THE GHOST OF A DEAD ANCESTOR IS WATCHING?

When moving from the living-room
to the kitchen $\qquad$ at night-time I
turn off the light
$\qquad$ fumble out of the lounge
$\qquad\qquad\qquad\qquad$ down the $\qquad$ hall &
into the kitchen $\qquad$ where I then
turn on the kitchen light &
$\qquad\qquad\qquad$ banish the darkness.

Most times
$\qquad$ I manage it
without bumping into things
$\qquad\qquad$ because really
there's not that many
$\qquad\qquad\qquad$ things
to bump into

AT THE END OF THE ROAD IS A HIGH WOODEN TOWER IN WHICH A MAN WITH A BIG GUN STANDS

The penis rises above magnolia suds
    like the periscope of some fleshy
submarine. I can almost feel
    the weight of your left breast
against my slippery lips, and almost
    hear the beating of your heart.
Blood-thud, breath rhythm
    powers this pen and page, provokes
the lonely thought of two people
    sitting as far apart as possible
on a park bench painted green.
    Only one of them wears a
gardenia in a button-hole.
    Only one of them
feeds birds with bits of bread.

INSOMNIA: 1ST NOVEMBER, 1993, 7:38 AM

This is when you think
your best lines will come;
mimetic bat, you soar with the dawn
through layers of blind space
grasping at bugs & blood & blackness
but all that boils is the kettle,
all that smoulders is the cigarette
burning blue in the dirty ashtray,

There is some logic here, if you could follow it,
but your mind, strafed by waking,
pataphysically stalls on the first rung
of the pebble;
self-reflectivity, pebble within pebble,
each beach harbours itself an infinity-fold,
cell within cell, endless helical,
no cell sleeps but sleep takes place within them.

The birds have stopped singing.
Lazarus still stands at the lip of his grave,
you can see the weighing taking place in his
zombie eyes,
his face pulled down with gravity, with
sadness,
hauled out of that safe sleep
which encapsulates every endlessness;
you can hear him asking with dirt in his throat
which was the better place to leave.
You can see him look longingly at the
mud in his fingernails,
see him caress the worms in his hair.

It's all bollocks. It's all just
nonsense words. 7:54. The house
awakes. Come forth,
because there are many
mucky and moneyed things to do today.

STORM

The hot air syrups the rain
before it hits
the ground

the parked cars
electrically havocked
herald the coming lightning
with their alarms

the startled squeals then
the flashing blue clamour

skeletal hands of giants
yanking at the sea

stilting along the coast
towards
the other clusters of lights

the hissing sea
just for an instant
bluer than you could ever imagine

this is Wales
but it could be anywhere

Guatemala
Madagascar
Peru

the whole planet
cooling
bowing to this driving rain
the blinding light

oh for it to stay like this
the sea, the hills
at hysterical pitch

you would open your face
to those
snatching vast hands

& never need the sun
or wait for the morning

again

NEWSNIGHT 1999

Bottles of Coca Cola
lifted off the shelves

Scientists clone first
human embryo

The Serb paramilitary
machine-gunned 50 people

24 of whom were children
all of whom were non-combatants

He finished off the survivors
with a hand-grenade

Now Serb civilians flee
fearing Albanian retribution

NATO soldiers and KLA
each have 100% control of the city

camouflage uniforms
tanks tear up roads

disturbed soil
and flies crawl on corpses

eyes in bags
facial bruising

burnt shells of houses
burnt shells of cars

cans of Coca-Cola flee burnt cities
three-fingered saluting embryo

run for their lives
through mountains, dirt roads

massacre fizz
faulty CO_2

effervescent embryo
finished off with a Cola grenade

American troops
DNA armed

It's all coming, you know
it's all coming

GETTING WET

& I see us now, 50 years on,
naked on a pebble beach,
hand-in-hand
in our sagging body-sacks
hobbling into the sea
& smiling,
our few teeth
blue in the moon.

See our tattoos
shapeless blue with age.
I see our walnut arses
disappearing
beneath the waves.

11:11:99: TOTAL ECLIPSE

People cling to the hill
like birds.

Darkness in the morning and
they stand
like ghosts.

In a vast shadow
they look and hum
like electric sentinels, they

stand graven-image still
and stare at the sky
like enraptured lovely
children, filled
once again
with wonder.

COLD CHICKEN MADRAS, 9 AM

I mean, he's
going on again
about how he's going to save up
buy a Harley
and a gun
and drive across south America.

I mean, just
him and his bike
and his gun.

I mean,
Mexico.

I mean,
Peru.

I mean,
Nicaragua.

I mean, sleepless
and having to listen to this
bullshit.

I mean, middle-class
whitey
with dreads.

I mean,
Bolivia.

I mean,
fuck off.

TEN YEARS ON

& I remember
the wall coming down
brick by painted brick

soldiers with guns
people cheering
in their thousands

how I waited for you
on the platform

your body & your hair
& how you smiled

history in my head

they were exciting times

MILLENNIUM NEWS

Liverpool lost
away at Spurs
and in Oxford
in the early hours of New Year's Day
thieves broke in
to the Ashmolean museum
and stole a Cezanne painting
worth several million pounds.
As Oxford celebrated
they were in there,
dark shapes gliding
through the fog
from smoke grenades,
explosions and cheering
around them.

Now the world
wakes up to a hangover
and one man
(and it's got to be one man)
stands looking
at the painted village,
the pretty white houses with
red-tiled rooves,
the trees.
Several million pounds' worth
of paint' good brush-strokes
in a good arrangement.

It's Tuesday tomorrow.
The world will return to work.

IN THE DOORWAY OF BARCLAY'S BANK

Stocking up for New Year's Eve
cigarettes
beer
whiskey
vodka
and the young man
in the doorway of Barclay's bank
in ragged jeans
on the cold marble step
stops me.
I delve
into my pocket for money
and he rolls his shirt-sleeve up
and says: - No, no, I don't want that,
I want you to see this...

There is a wound on his forearm,
deep maroon slash,
weeping and ferocious.
I say: - I don't want to see it, man,
just take the fucking money ,
and press the coins
into his hand.

I mean,
I've got bags to carry.
I've been there as well.
There's shopping to be done.
It's New Year's Eve 1999
and there isn't much time left.

AND THE STORY OF US ALL IS AN ONGOING ONE

Last night
it rained
& I slept
with the blanket edge
tucked tight
between the cheeks of my arse,
so when I awoke
one buttock was hot
& the other icy cold.
The cleft was just the
right temperature.

& my first thought
on waking
was: Captain Eddie Rickenbacker,
American World War One
flying ace.

What he saw.
What he did.

I'll never
know why.

NOW I'M FREE

It's not like it's disappointing, or
anything like that; not like it
lets me down, or falls short

of the promises I made for it.
It's just that, somehow,
there are things still here
I imagined
would flee; the sudden tears
burning
on a sunny afternoon
when a song
just for a moment
achieves an arrangement of notes
& turns into a spear.
It's just that
I didn't think
the heart
would remain so black,
or the panic
still roil.
Or that the dreams would stay so vile,
so horrendous, so sickening, or
the urge to buy that gun
& do everybody else the favour
I've always thought should be done.

But
fuck it all, fuck
it all; there is food there is booze
there are no bailiffs. There
are things
I'm free from
now.

DRIVING AROUND TOWN

D's at the wheel
cos I can't drive
I'm checking out the feet
of a girl in sandals
a pedestrian a PEDESTRIAN
& we stop at a zebra
& the girl crosses
which is a result
my eyes behind shades
the sun beats & burns & batters
the parched town
& comes back off the sea
in amber shrapnel
& the tourists waddle pinkly
or most of them do
our car our CAR
first one I've ever owned
or part-owned
& we in it
me & my lovely woman
the mountains are friendlier
the sea is kinder
clink of bottles behind
& the humming sun
& us in the exhaust fumes
& our new fun

CHEAP DAY RETURN TO THE PALACE OF WISDOM

Teeth grinding before we leave Llangollen
the babbling begins
& some old heads turn
did we sleep
one hour or two? How much have we drunk?
How much MDMA did we do
& how much speed
strange stuff it was
intense whizz hit that dissipated after half an hour
characteristic of charlie
but a tenner a bag just
& the recess behind the Nissan hut
which became sodden with piss
& the high wall we sat on
the treacherous high wall
the moths around the light
& the bats around the moths
& all the bulging eyes
two hours ahead of us
on this bus
& it takes us home through the hills
as the night falls
passengers frozen in yellow light
like gnats in amber
& we grind our teeth
& we talk crap
& the bus takes us over the hills
towards our home
following the river
a lead thread through the trees
the stars come out
& we're happy

NAMELESS

My splendid secret

you groan and you come
like nobody else

us in a pub
beer with amphet chasers

sucking your nipples
you sucking mine

my balls in your mouth

the taste of your anus
just two days that went too quickly

my splendid secret

the robin's nest
in the heart of the cave

your fingers clutching my skull
tightly, tightly

my splendid secret
you shine from these walls
like spilled sperm
or tears,
pure,
wonderful,
& entirely impossible to erase

MY JESUS

I don't need you
when the money runs out
(then I just need money)
or the food or the fuel
or anything else like that
but when the light dies
      I feel you
here & here & here
      inside me;
my eyes   my breast   my hands
my balls   my guts   my brain.

So that's easy; loving you,
then,
is just loving a part of myself.

That's what makes it easy.
Yet
at a dawn kitchen table
when no birds sing
& my tongue is furred
with drink & tobacco
& my brain is buzzing with drugs,

then when I sit empty,

there is no
love
in the world
      like mine.

RAIN IS POISON & SEX IS DEATH

In rusty buckets of stagnant rainwater
& in the mould on teabags
      left to rot behind the bin,

in oil-slicked puddles & stained
chip-papers on Sunday mornings,

in burst pimples & mucus,
in the craters of the moon
& the peaks of the sea,

it seems I can see your face,
its smile of vapid panic
& barely-controlled hysteria,

& in the industrial sprawls of belief & faith
this contributes only
more waste & pollution,
more geese falling limp-winged through smog,

the stink of kerosene on skin
impossible to wash off,
lost, aimless,

there you are & there,
desultory, idiopathic,
here to stay & impossible to avoid.

This is a generation that knows little else; to
make love could be fatal,
to enjoy a spring rain on your face

could mean blindness, psoriasis, impetigo,
ageing.
Well, what do you do; you
eat
& watch TV
& masturbate
& roar
& find somebody, anybody,
to refuse to forgive. It's
easy.

JUST LIKE THE BLIND MAN REQUIRES HIS GUIDE-DOG; JUST LIKE THE ORCHIDS REACH FOR THE SUN

Little sparrow
with the twig in your beak
it's always you that I think of
when, after sex, me and my lover
              lying together
(sticky with sweat,
my front to her back, my left knee
nuzzling her thigh, my right arm
flung over, hand curved around breast,
my right leg on top of hers, my left
arm raveled into my neck, my head
tilted back to avoid tickling hair, my
wilting penis resting between slippery
arsecheeks)
I notice that
a wafer of light
shines from the hall

underneath the bedroom door,
and I am absolutely positive
that I extinguished all lights
before we both, smiling,
crept into bed,
45 minutes or so
ago.

TO ALL MY FELLOW PRISONERS

Siblings in guilt;
please don't worry
about the dirt on your skin,
the blood and the mucus
staining your clothes;
that's simply the sign
that he
who created you from clay
is merely preparing
to call you back
into his
welcoming, warm and
(you know it)
wished-for arms.

FOOD

All day
the sea
has been vile in its fury
seen in a new light
until 5AM

light from a hovering helicopter
lifeboat searchlight
pub searchlight

she was snatched from the beach
just past midnight
into the whiskery warty
liverspotted waves

which still today
all day
belch and break on the pebbles
spit stones onto the promenade
fart at Ireland

her body still unfound.

Another lost one
eyed now by crab carapace
wigged with bladderwrack
just another lost one
pickled pure in brine

may you make
a mighty meal
lovely enough to appease
such vile ungrateful rage

YOU'RE WISHING YOUR FUCKING LIFE AWAY, MAN

The concrete wall
was two feet thick
eight feet high & ten wide
reinforced with a skeleton
of tensile steel
bombproof

it protected
amongst other works
the original manuscript of
The Canterbury Tales
&
The Black Book of Carmarthen

the boss
wanted it down.
We had
three jackhammers

a small one
about a foot long
which was as
useful
as a toothpick

a medium blue one
which bounced in your arms
like a wildcat
& was
therefore

useless too
& a huge bastard
75 pounds
strong as a tank
& labelled
THOR

this was the one
we favoured
heavy & unwieldy
but with a man
at each handle
it gulped & tore
the concrete away
roaring
battering belching thing
us ramming it
into the wall
balanced on
loose-plank trestles

taming it
ripping the wall away in chunks
exposing the steel
& then
hacking that away
with a grinder
in a
screeching shower of sparks

we'd pick
THOR up
at eight thirty
in the morning

after a half hour spent
filling the
generator with diesel
& put him down again
at five, five thirty, six o clock
our hands frozen
into claws
every muscle
screaming
tendons cracking
bones rubbing raw
ears almost bloody
hacking
up gelatinous grey
jellyfish
of dust & mucus

home
bath
eat bed.

Three pounds an hour
beginning at eight
the following morning

I asked the brickie
working nearby
what time it was

five fuckin minutes since you last
asked
you're wishing your fucking life away
man

which was true
but
worse; I've
never
wished for anything
quite so much or
desperately.

When we finally
after two months of this
blasted away
the final lump of concrete
& stood
shaking
in the hole we'd made
I felt
not one tiny
jolt or thrill
of triumph
or fulfillment.
Not
one

MAD JANET RAFFERTY

Ah, the children; like
little chirpy jackdaws,
always running and
singing, darting here
and there, no time to rest,
more life now, always
chasing after the

brightest, prettiest
tinkle or bauble.
God love them; they
need someone to.

> Her bones were found
> in the ruins after the fire
> had been put out, bared
> and blackened, the jaw
> unhinged and toothless.
> No-one ever
> found out who she was.

BWLCH

it's like
immense green bodies
in a repose large enough
to plug the gaps
in any life and
an even huger sky
hangs over this

sheep in the foreground
can anchor the restless
bewildered
gulping eye
a hillocky maggot-mad fleece
only serves to stretch
the smile of this stone god

stand alone

amongst all this
vast still space
and you are colossal
fecund
and full

DON'T EVEN THINK ABOUT IT

you'll never find me
ashamedly spewing
into a dirty toilet

you'll never see me
weeping uncontrollably
on an airport runway

you'll never hear me
screaming for help
from the mouth of a cave

because I have been
the parasite
in the antler of the snail

I have been
the flesh shred
trapped in the teeth of the tiger

I have been
the lint
in everybody's belly-button

and I will always win

ADVICE

Brian, the fork-lift driver,
tells me over
his
one o' clock pork pie
that I
should try to
write for a
living.
Anyone can do it, he says.
All you have to do is paint,
                paint with words.

He points to the river
which flows past the warehouse,
carries the sewage
from the store's canteen
out to the sea.
I mean, look at that, he says.
*Just look at what you see and paint
it
in words .*

Well, alright;
the river is lillied
by carrier bags
and the store sells,
amongst many other things,
decorative doorplates
and clips to hold plants
to climbing rods.

Brian once
had an article about geese
published
in a magazine somewhere.

I eat my sandwiches
sit in the sun
and smoke
for an hour

and then go back inside
to shift boxes
and ascertain
that boil-coloured shower curtains
('Misty Pink', it says on the label)
are
priced correctly.

WOULD YOU CONSIDER GOING OUT WITH AN ALIEN?

You fucking arsehole.
Hold this cunt down, Mick,
I'll sort this fucker out...
Oof.
No more nappies to change for you,
now, ey?
I see the gratitude
spurting from your ears...

Like need
& success,
gratitude is red;
a red glue
to re-set
the wings of clipped birds.

Hold er steady there now...
Fetch the fucking gardening shears.
Smile, lad, smile;
Christ I'd sue that fucking dentist
if I was you.
I saw a UFO once.
It hovered over me
on the beach
& then took off at
an impossible angle at
an unbelievable speed.

Stamp on the fucker's hands,
harder, lad, HARDER!

Budgies sing.
My roses need pruning.

JUST LIKE I'VE ALWAYS DREAMED

Like getting the short end of the wishbone
or pulling a Christmas cracker & there's
    nothing inside;
like peeling a potato when you're
    hungry hungry hungry

& finding it black with eyes beneath the skin;
like asking the cashpoint machine for money
with a thirst as scorched as Saharan sand
& you get   SORRY: THERE ARE
INSUFFICIENT FUNDS IN YOUR ACCOUNT.

It's always like this.
No, it's worse; you wear
disappointment like shoes,
you take it to the shop to buy
milk & cigarettes, it's
not merely something
that will occupy you
for a lone evening
when you're not alone
or for the time it takes you
to eat breakfast
& brush your teeth
while your partner lies sleeping.

It's something that will lay
your drowsy head on the pillow
& stand by your bedside as you slumber.
It will guide you into wakefulness,
crusted around your tearducts,
a discharge the colour of cheap margarine.

IF I HEARD HER CALL MY NAME

When nothing much happens
when the moon does not shine red
when the killing still continues

& the waves refuse to sing
when feet still stink
& the semen seethes
& bed is only a place to re-fuel
that's when you hear it
that's when it happens:

the bawling
the baying
the loud howling
far inside
deep inside.

I think I'd think about it, though;
I'd carry on with my everyday activities
& think about it long & hard
before dropping everything like Ming china
& running in that direction
as fast as furious as I fucking could
without even stopping to
say goodbye

A LITTLE DROP OF MOISTURE ON A PACKET OF RIZLAS & YOU LOSE THE WHOLE FUCKING LOT

Ireland might not get through
    to the world cup 2nd round.
The pipe in the yard
may never stop dripping.

The corn is blighted,
the livestock is leprous;

this morning's paper
crumbles like an Egyptian bandage.

What was the helicopter looking for
last night, stuttering above my house?

The clouds bloom black with rain.

Of course there is a point in angels. Jesus.

SCREAMING BLUE MURDER

Why?
Why that particular phrase
for that particular action?
Why not red? Why not yellow?
Euphemism? Metaphor? Synecdoche?
What pictures does it throw up
in your head?

Ah, if you can explain that
you'll be able to bear it
the next time that person
looks at you & it seems as if
not them but
Agamemnon
is using
their eyes
for that moment.

SO THE RUN-OVER CATS CAN PROWL GRACEFULLY INTO HEAVEN

Writing in the yard with
the sun on my nape,
steady time-keeping of water
and a bit muttering behind the houses,
blue sky blue sky there's no point in
yearning for what you can't have; the
sea still stutters at the foot of the road,
no butter then use margarine
and a sharp knife to hone your pencil;
like light brown dogs with grinning eyes
and a couple hand-in-hand so old that
they could be dead, the patience
of a spider in its red, webbed heart
is the perfect calm before the storm;
praying for rain so the Namib might sing,
soothing the broken heart of a starling;
just watch the small birds
wind-flicked away from the ridge of the roof
peering out of the greasy window at dawn
with the sleeping partner behind you,
the two of you walking midnight streets
while the baffling and confusing universe
continues all around; no clean underwear,
don't wear any, fumble for tobacco
and settle for tea; there will continue
to be faces drifting out of the fog
for as long as you are allowed to live,
greet them love them kiss them smash them -
it is worth living for,
wonderful, and wise,
like the setting free of eagles.

FLEA-BITE

All waiting
is staring at a stagnant pond
in the scummed edges of which
float
a child's red wellington boot
an empty Sunblest wrapper
a dead pigeon
an empty tin can
with
the colours bleached
away

WITH YOUR HAND OUT THE WINDOW NO-ONE CAN TELL WHETHER YOU'RE SEIZING THE DAY OR WAVING GOODBYE

Yes, yes, OK, yours was worse,
& I would never have exchanged
my war for yours
but God that one was & still is mine
& I'll crush it against my breast
        for ever;

the clinic's sign in the neatly-trimmed
hedgerows, I remember the nose-bleeds
the alcoholics eating dubbin sandwiches
the screams, the banging of faces
needing heroin
against unsympathetic brick,

needle-tracks & vaginas
diarrhea was my mustard gas
blood was my blood
tears were my tears
my face in the morning
as constant as shell-fire
but always reflected
in different surfaces

& why did I laugh so much

The friendly nurses
the suicidal friends
all still alive
(but I don't know about the nurses)

The taste of brandy & sulphate
for breakfast
when there'd been no sleep
only
a vague drifting
between sheets
with unfamiliar smells

razor-blade vade mecum

lying in the bath in boxer shorts
newly-bought
a bottle of whisky
a Wilkinson Sword double-edged
the bathwater cluttered with roses & sperm

& you were always a soft place to land on
laughing in the beer gardens
bee-loud
late-night ice-cream parlours
trousers ripped at the crotch

Shitting myself in the shopping centre
walking like a cowboy to the nearest public toilet
buses buses
why were there always buses
oh
& pigeons too
one dead blackbird
& one dead tramp
slumped in the alleyway
we dragged his lips up into a smile
& stuck a lit cigarette between them
his flesh like plasticine
unknown dead man
that was a cold winter &
you're here still
between my ribs
you laugh when I breathe & my lungs expand

Boiled potatoes & LSD
waking up with my face as big as the pillow
loose teeth, black eyes
swollen lips painful to drink through

police cars police stations
my face on security cameras

sweaty in a kitchen now
I never dreamed of then

I remember you
both enemy & friend

All this it was
this more
my war my lover my friend my pen
my dove bringing an olive branch
over the wilding waves
I'm glad you're still here
you demand one last plea
because you know
as sure as the fucking sun
I'll gladly give it to you

don't ever go
don't ever leave
pray every night that you'll never ever end

TRUTH

'I don't know, it's
like they all seem to
want the same thing,
their faces go all slack when they come,
they all want to go afterwards,
mostly it's crap
and I think is that it?
They all seem to want the same thing'.

And, later:

'come here & let me clean your face,
you've got ink all over it.
You're all such little children.
You all need looking after'.

VISITING WHITTINGTON

For a few minutes
past midnight
travelling back to Wales from Yorkshire

there were ducks in Whittington
on the lake in Whittington
so very quiet
the stars in the water
so still

a castle with a house inside
& several thatched & sleeping pubs

little border town
I think I would love to live in you
you must harbour no treacheries
conceal no cowardice
moated you must be against murder
& pain

the ducks have flown to you

people will kiss on your green heart

inside your cottages
are fresh cakes & tea
& smiling grandmothers in aprons
who smell of milk
& want nothing more
than my perfect happiness

I would crunch through the snow to the shop
walk past the castle
buy bread & cheese & fruit & cigarettes
& return home to a log fire & a book & an armchair
& a wholly insurmountable cat

frustration-free Whittington
how strong your locks would be
no booze, no drugs
in Whittington

nesting there are barn-owls & badgers
war veterans with brilliant tales

I would visit the pubs
to buy amphetamine & weed
& get drunk
& scrabble for sex
no I wouldn't

safe from bombs
& red tape
& faceless brown envelopes
on the morning doormat
no bruises there
or vomiting
or screaming

no weeping in Whittington
or needing
or pleading

you are not a ghost-town
but no doubt you have ghosts

I know you have ghosts

you have a castle
& ducks
& water
& sky
& houses
 & pubs
& ghosts

SALLY REDWINE

Maddening in your aloofness
slightly frightening in your hunger

we'd sit from opening until closing
drinking marathon pints of bitter and stout
and then you'd give up drinking and
sex like a good Catholic girl

you hated your stepmother

sometimes I would sit
behind the door of my room
and wait to hear you return

just me a need and a bottle
and some nights you never did

you cried many times
I bought you many flowers
and once I hit you in the face
with a bean-bag

you would jangle keys
and you had brown eyes

a nose broken
from falling off a horse
when very young

Sally
Sally
it was never a mistake
and I'm sorry

sometimes I still miss you
and always I remember your laugh

your teeth

the smell of you
like a baby
the veins in the backs of your hands
as you gave me the directions to a pub
I'd never been to

your fingernails walking
across the counter-top
in that filthy kitchen

you crushed my head
when you came
as I was licking you

the tea you would make of a morning
your interminable baths
gritting my teeth
when I came across your back

your persistence in things
the sadness in you
I knew it you told me

your breasts
the biggest I'd ever held
or kissed or sucked or tumbled into
the delicate tracery
of big blue veins

your soft tummy
your laughter

wine spilled across your carpet
licking yoghurt off your ribs
kicking the pot over
spilling the remainder
your accent
and your snarl

your beautiful lips

all those years ago Sally
it didn't last long enough Sally
not a wish to extend it Sally

but to have it begun earlier

We fell in love, Sally
but not with each other

yet still sitting here
writing this
another one two rooms away
and you are still
Sally Redwine
and much
much more

LOVELY DIRTY NASTY BRUTAL UGLY FUCKED-UP GORGEOUS WORLD

Sun nourishes the mud
from the mud springs algae
the algae beckons the fish
& the fish call forth puffins
      the puffins nest & lay
inviting the hawks & foxes
      & life explodes

steppe eagles brawling over the matted
corpse of a flamingo

if I could stroke a swan's neck
& bury my face in its breast
then I could forget you
& your absence

from a distance
the planet is blue

I'd let you stand & watch
as my back disappeared beneath the bird's wings
& you'd be able to see me smile & purr
& with your lovely eyes observe
my face relax
as I pushed the shrapnel of the memories of you
out through muscle out through skin
& away into the air

I wouldn't want it
any
other
way

REPEATS

Lunch-time
I'm watching
History File
a programme for schools
about America's war
in Vietnam

I've seen this before,
how many years ago,
four?, five?,
under similar circumstances,
waiting for a woman to

come home
from university
for the day

Ah, how it all comes back,
all the images of suffering,
the forests leafless, greenless
the panic & the flame
the skin sloughing off in slabs

maybe
in 1998
it will all happen again -
different woman
different place
same programme
& me

I am, right now, well-fed
I am recovering from a speed binge
I am feeling horny
& apprehensive

this pen waits to run out of ink
as
planets wait to align

HAIKU: PONYTAIL

Little squirrel
perched on your shoulder
whispering secrets   in your ear

HAIR OF AUBURN WATER

They're hauling someone out
of a canal in Venice
& they're slowly swinging
side-to-side
& upside-down

flies gather
as do people
the hauling apparatus hums

the body is either male or female
naked but dressed in pallid sludge
& it sways silently
beneath grey sky

its flesh threatens to slide off in slabs
& everybody on the canal banks
will talk later
in the cafes & bars
about its wonderful auburn hair

THE LUCKIEST MAN IN THE WORLD

He's on the news;
a paraglider
who fell over a mile to earth
when his emergency 'chute
failed to open.

He's alive,
alive
with several crushed vertebrae
shattered leg
broken foot
& dark eyes
which
stare
into the endless distance
inches
before his nose.

Imagine it,
though;
the slow fall
through
weightless
softness,
wind whistling
in your ears,
time
enough
to dwell
on what
this plunge,
plummet, will
teach you.
And, now,
the abundant vastness
everywhere,
everywhere;

between each word
each touch

each slice of
every sandwich.

All that space; just
the birds
& you.

Lucky fucker.

AFTER A GLORIOUS DREAM OF FUCKING FOUR WOMEN

Toast
& tea
&
now
what?

A strange loss...

A cool sea wind
comes through
the open window

it is four days
until I get
any money

& I am down
to dry & brittle
crumbs of tobacco

I need
bread
margarine
toilet paper
vinegar
cheese
some vegetables
a new pair of jeans

I owe the man
in the shop
2 pound
for yesterday's newspapers

I have 4 pound
until Friday

I sit here
staring at the walls.

Such an odd, flimsy
yet still stubbornly pervasive
sense of loss,
sore &
unwanted...

Christ. They
were so vivid.

ANSWERING BACK

Oi, you, twat -
don't you fucking dare
tell me
what
happens when I die

I know what happens
when I die

all the mistakes
I've ever made

will be paraded before me
in a long long
line
& I'll be forced
to choose
just one
as my eternal coffin-mate

&
that's just in
Heaven

LIVING

drinking tea
looking out the window
for one woman
to return,
I smell the cunt
of another
on my fingers
every
time
I raise toast
to my
mouth

SCRATCHING

this chewed biro
against this clean paper
makes tiny gnawing noises
scratching sounds
little insect legs
on glass
insistent
brilliant
huge disobedient howl

that's what this
is this
writing this
thing to do
with words

giant v sign
to the shrieking warplane this
safety of a warm and quiet pub
on a winter afternoon, this
silver slap of the waves

this machine-gun
when you're cornered
in an alley   this
twenty pound note
in an envelope   this
talkative tomcat   this
iced lager
by the sea
on a hot summer day   this

is fucking beautiful

MY NEW BOOTS

are huge
chunky
iron-cleated   buckled
two tanks
on my legs

they could kick down bank vaults
start a revolution
smash down the
Berlin Wall
if it was still there

when I walk down
the street in them
I am empowered   mighty
they cause large dogs to flee
& old ladies
to tut in
disapproval

stomping across the varnished
wooden floors of pubs
they boom with each step
& rattle the pumps & fonts
on the bar

ten feet tall I am
an actor in a Greek chorus
a stripey spider
spinning his web
a rat leaping six feet
straight up
towards your throat

they are my new boots
they are mine

E#1

in the hope of something
that ought to last
& not self-destruct

mist on the mountains
& in the back of a car
the E
comes on

impossible to convey
just
happy
happy
happy

clinging to the bumper
yet still whisked away
by the
wonderful whirlwind

not scared
now of what I
am what I'm
not what
might become
what I might
not become

this glorious gamble
pays off once again

impossible to convey
just
fucking gorgeous
run
towards
the flashing
lights

SAD

It's okay
it's quite simple,
really; just, you
know, let that
little throb
insist on
itself, let it
be
there.

God, it could be worse; it's
only a promise of
restless sleep &
minutes wasted
in blankness. That's
all.

It's not, for
instance, the ugly
seed which will
sprout into the
hideous tree in

whose crone-
knuckled branches
you'll one day
sling your
noose.

It could be worse.

SUNDAY DRUNK

the newspapers
& cold white wine
& sun
& house music
loud & hypnotic
which is how it should be

how it all should be

I feel fine as fuck
nothing's wrong
it's all okay

a gorgeous way
to waste a day

DEAD DOG DREAMS

He comes to me in the form, usually,
of a friendly middle-aged man; a
barman, say, or a postman with a
parcel.
He says that I don't have
to worry about him; that
he has lots to do -
rubber bones the size of trees,
bags of chocolate like pillow-cases,
cats with no claws who run.
He tells me he never catches them.

He had,
he says,
the best life he ever could've wished for;
he says that that,
along with his present condition,
is a minor miracle.

He says that now, where he is,
there's no waiting;
no howling;
& he can shit anywhere he wants.

He says that
it's one immense green field
where he can run
& run
& run.

He says not to worry.
It's okay, he says,
being dead.

WHEN YOU READ THIS

you'll
wonder where I am

whether I'm dead
whether I'm happy
lonely
taking a bath
swinging from a bough
in an ignored forest
belly-up
in some dark mountain lake

in love
alone
drinking with friends
hunting purple seagulls
where   you'll wonder
where
& only I'll know

so there.
Another futile,
totally useless
victory

THE GENIUS

It was strange
he had it all -
the dress (non)sense,
the wilding hair,
the drink habit,
the way of looking
at everyday objects
with a childish wonder
as if seeing them
for the first time...

He lived off women
who supported him gladly
in gratitude for his sexual
prowess and wit
and badinage
and his striding up and down the kitchen
declaiming to them
on Sunday evenings.

He loved animals
he couldn't cook
or pay his bills

and he moved back in
with his mum and dad
when he was 37.

Everybody waited
for his first great book
his magnum opus
his *Wasteland*
his. . .

Yet, apart from a few scribbles
in obscure periodicals
which sunk rapidly without a ripple
the genius remained
unpublished.

Gradually, interest
waned in him;
he inherited the house
when his parents died
and became just another
cardiganned bumbler,
drinking cheap whisky
and pruning his roses.

When he died, the
social services
(he never sired)
emptied his house;
they found drawers
stuffed full of words,
poems, essays, novels, plays,
thousands of them,
a lifetime's worth,

which they read
and thought mildly diverting
then threw
in the incinerator.

And that
was it.

12/09/1996: THREE OH

No more
looking forward to the date
no more
unexpected presents or excitement
no
bottles of ouzo before noon
no
energy to keep on going

no more
older women who say
for such a young lad, you're an amazing fuck

no more
adult expressions
which declare
bemused tolerance
because of youth

no
constant and consuming jealousies
over previous boyfriends

no
insistence
on being the centre
of every personal world

no more tattoos

no more
desire to roar and run
until all eyes are on me

no more
strings of wilfully sleepless nights
perhaps
no more
weeping
at songs
or TV programmes

no
watching the sea for hours on end
in the hopes
of seeing a fin
or a blow-hole

no questions like:
where are you going
for how long and who with
what time will you be back

and no more
fury
at the lack of
answer

being peurile
and petulant, and
revelling in that
being the first to snort
and the last to
sleep, the quickest to
snarl, the facility
for weeping, the
constant hard-on, the
bizarre and terrifying dreams

no more, ever
again, this is
adulthood

DRYING OUT

Aye, well, sometimes
these things
happen
the urge just leaves
but you know
like writing
the next day, line,
will produce
something different,
the fingers working
ahead of the brain
and the brain
catching up
with things unthought
unwilled

they just appear

and for some reason
I'm remembering
a delicatessen
in Cambridge
where I used to buy
wine and halva
late at night

you daft cunt,
Griffiths, you're
fucking well
drunk
again

POOR

I will count out my 2p's and 1p's
I will put them into plastic bags
(£1 of 1's, £1 of 2's, £1 of mixed)
I will take them to the bank
and exchange them for coins of higher
denomination
I will go to the supermarket
I will buy potatoes, margarine, fish-fingers
I will come home
and I will eat

ALL OF THIS, ONLY

sorry
because of the blood

terrified, haunted
sleep robbed by hysterical dreams
because of the blood

a liking for rain
because of the blood

see betterness in animals
their small-eyed self-absorption
because of the blood

sing loudly when drunk
find it difficult to avoid giving insult
because of the blood

can find excuses
because of the blood

can fall into sadness
purely by accident
because of the blood

have massive needs
and huge hopes
because of the blood

always want more
because of the blood

feel refusal as terrifying
as the rotten black potatoes
dug up on the long-ago rainy morning
because of the blood

want
because of the blood

fight the ever-present
need to apologise
because of the blood

think about hiding in the mountains
as I'm running mad through cities
because of the blood

find the planet both beautiful and appalling
and much of the life on it ugly and pointless
and filled with wonder
because of the blood

seek out solitude
and then in it yearn for friends
because of the blood

puzzled
because of the blood

need too much
because of the blood

hate
because of the blood

make a twat of yourself at parties
because of the blood

eat soup
because of the blood

stare at a blank wall
because of the blood

draw attention
by any means
because of the blood

fight
because of the blood

lie and steal
because of the blood

find your face collapsing in grief
because of the blood

let wonder become anger
let questing become frustration
because of the blood

be terrified of rotten fruit
because of the blood

strive to give a shape to the future
and when this is finally achieved
find it unattractive
because of the blood

dig
because of the blood

and delight
because of the blood

and despise
because of the blood

and die
because of the foul fucking pumping blood

ANOTHER MUGGY NIGHT

through the open window
comes the sound of something
screaming   a small mammal or
bird, caught in the claws or
jaws of a larger mammal or
bird. Thinking it may be the
wheezing of air in my face I
hold my breath and
listen hard; the screaming goes on,
climbs up into desperation, suddenly
stops. I smoke a cigarette, run a bath,
write this. Obvious, really; how we are
all preoccupied with screaming in the
darkness, howling for a help which
never even offers to come

DON'T ANSWER THE DOOR, IGNORE THE PHONE

Stay inside; within these four walls
you can be whoever you want to be,
as heroic
or pathetic
as you've always dreamed -
you can stride across the kitchen
with your chest puffed out,
you can stare into the mirror
and weep, you can fall to your knees
in cheaply-carpeted bedrooms
or drown yourself in tea.
At nine o' clock
the wind brings salt
through the open window and
cats prowl the corridor
to seek you out,
darkness falls as you decide
which particular shit to watch
on the tv.
Sleep lurks like a spider.
Books hum. Here you are
safe; inside you are wrapped
in promises, untouchable,
invincible; God-like amongst dust,
turning somersaults
above the fridge
while Mir continues
to spin forever
in space.

LIKE SOME HALF-REMEMBERED NIGHTMARE

Christmas 1998
& Aberystwyth was snowed in.
The sea broke sluggish
against a vast dirty pillow
scribbled with greasy hair.
& the wolf came down
from beyond Pen Dinas
in search of food; grey &
scrawny, slat-ribbed & high-
shouldered, it nuzzled the
bins behind the Belle Vue
& found turkey bones & cold
sprouts & cabbage, pudding &
curdled brandy butter; had
the streets not been deserted,
there would have been screaming &
running, people hiding in their houses,
barricading their doors & windows
& huddling in the fires' circle of
warm protection
against threat & fear & shadow.
The wolf sloped
past their windows & doors
& they caught a whiff of secret
carnage & huddled closer to the heat of
coal or gas or electric charge.
The smell tickled their scalps.
The wolf ate a housecat
on the giant bed of the bowling green,
stood on hind legs
with his paws on the sill

& peered through a window
at a fat man sleeping off gluttony.
Silently the wolf pissed against a car
& stuck his tongue out to taste the snow.
Down Vaynor Street
Thomas Morgan, a First World War veteran
& the oldest man in Dyfed,
rushed out into the street
in his pyjamas
& shot the wolf at close range; there
was neither yelp nor blood
as the animal collapsed into a snow-drift.
The police surrounded Thomas
& ordered him to drop his weapon; he
wouldn't, & appeared to be in a very
excited & agitated state, so the police
shot him too. He died & was buried
with full military honours.
When the snow thawed, no wolf corpse
was found; only the stiff, blue
mannequin of a 17-year-old junkie
at the bottom of Pen Dinas,
the syringe still stuck in his arm.

MAYBE IT'S DIFFERENT IN SWEDEN

Sometimes
it comes at night; a silent
swarm
of stubborn hornets
fizzing in my brain, a
bear on its back legs

breathing foul air in my face.
It just
forms itself out of the darkness.
Typed pages
are sent out in envelopes,
never to be seen again.
I am a fly
smashing my brains against
glass,
the whirring of wings
like laughter
at the futility
of word
following
word, & I will
continue to do
this
until I die.

DIAZEPAM

I dreamt that I
was Death

in a field of golden wheat

you couldn't see my feet
because my cloak
brushed the floor

you couldn't see my face
because my hood
covered it entirely

I stood in the corn
clasping my scythe

& heard
the wind
whistling through the stalks

the birds
singing in the trees

& everything
was
perfect

I THINK I NEED TO GET OUT MORE

tourists
in the baking sun
clog the promenade
turn pink
stand gawping at gaps in shops
get drunk and dance
like arseholes
in the pubs

one of them   today   just
stood there and ignored my
three excuse me's   but my one
will you gerrout the fucking way
was met with a spin
and a snarl
and muttered instructions to his mates

they squared up
glowered
and I came home.

Now, at
midnight   I hear
behind the welcome rain a
roaring at the
bottom of the road   I
take a crap
grab my largest and sharpest knife
sit down facing the door
and wait

PASTA BAKE

last night I rode
a laughing brontosaur
through the canyons
of New York
the people pointed and
gawped and smiled in
wonder   I waved my
stetson at the secretaries
at their computer screens
on the sixteenth floors

I loved my massive dinosaur   I
never saw his face   being
on his back and clinging to his
tree-trunk neck   but his
skin was greeny-gold and soft

to the touch like satin or
how a butterfly's wing
might feel if you were allowed
to stroke its bright colours
without causing damage
and robbing it of flight

RUBBING THE LAMP

if a man came through the door
with his eyes rimmed with blood
wearing a terry-cloth dressing-gown
his hair on fire
& carrying a gun

then me, my rat & the spiders
would all have
something to write
about

WHEN STARS HUM LIKE BAD RECEPTION

There's a man in Leicester
going prematurely bald
in the mirror he appears stuffed
his eyes dead behind a leather mask

& a boy
plays with his mongrel dog
across a field of snow

Christmas baubles shed their glitter
& Everglade alligators go
nowhere

that this skin can be used for furniture
or decoration
that murder tells us
more than anything else
ever could

the wind moulds coffins
out of the sand-dunes

& behind factories
in nettles
in crisp-bags behind Tesco's
a girl's knickers
are pulled down
& just for a few minutes
there is at least one person on this planet
who feels no fucking terror

RAISING ABERYSTWYTH

And as I slept I dreamed of a place
always surrounded by snow-topped mountains,
where wolves prowl lean and hungry
and overturn dustbins at midnight,
of a bedroom
with a quilted bed by the window
through which owls peer,
of a working harbour, seagull-speckled,

and the smell of weed and fish,
of a white-haired old couple
greeting their children and grandchildren
on Sunday mornings
when church bells ring
and kitchens smell of tea and cake,
of a shop
that sells everything
from anchovies to zit-cream
with a beaming white-smocked proprietor
very easy with his credit,
of an infinitely friendly and gentle priest
genuflecting over the trawlers
as they head out to sea
with their decks scrubbed clean
surrounded by leaping dolphins,
of a place with no boils or gout or flu,
of a garden green and vegetabled, with
the small green explosions of lettuce and cabbage,
of low bright clouds,
of steep cobbled streets,
of a calmness and a peace
and a tranquility too deep
for a heartbeat to die in.

I don't know; maybe it's
Ipswich.

SHOCK UPON SHOCK UPON SHOCK

as he waited in the rain
at the side of the road
for a gap in the traffic
it struck him that
war might be similar; large chunks
or metal and glass
filled with a liquid highly flammable
hurtling past him
at high speeds
close enough to cool his skin
and snatch at his thin and flimsy clothes.

Yet he did not tremble
or weep. Nor
did he start diving for cover
whenever he heard the word
truck.

IF FAIRIES CAN BE SQUEEZED FROM A BOTTLE

coming back to a dark & empty flat
after washing dishes for five hours,
sore and smelly at the feet,
soaked with soapy water at the chest,
hips
thighs
I make toast
& boil water
eject some uninvited spiders
crap

make a shopping list &,
as I write 'potatoes', I
am suddenly reminded
of the ribcage
of a girl called Susie; completely
& clearly I remember it,
how fragile it seemed,
how pronounced when she lay on her back
with her arms over her head,
my ear between her breasts
listening to her heart thud.

I write 'onions'.
I write 'milk',
'bread', & make a list
of debts to pay.

I eat my toast
drink my tea
and leave the dirty dishes in the sink
until morning.

This seems
to mean some-
thing.

WEDNESDAY

having paid with a twenty pound note
he left the shop
with a spade
an axe
a crowbar
and a length of sturdy chain

he stood at the bus-stop for ten minutes
then, changing his mind
boarded one southbound
through the city
through the suburbs
and out
to the bland housing estate
on the banks of the
rotten
canal

STORM WARNING

mad towels flap in the yard
a swarm of ghosts
shrieking & raging
at the windows

forces clash in the torn
& fleecy sky

floods in
Llanrwst
Barmouth

flying slates slice
sounds of whipping

falling like blades
catching the light
gunmetal light

windows tremble in their frames
the whole house shakes

the sea a cauldron boiling
with rage & hate

the wind is a threshing machine
driven by pure fury

property damage
dangerous conditions
all down the
east coast

light is shredded
& thrown into the air
the enraged air
to swirl like confetti

floods in
Cardigan
Rhondda valley

a 25 year old boy
was swept off the
promenade yesterday
& drowned

so far three
others
have been
killed

DEAD DOG

nothing happened
when he died, just
the needle went in
his heart stopped beating
& that was it – no
rush of air
as his soul departed
no shift in the world
as his molecules
began to reassemble themselves
into something not dog

he just lay there
growing colder
eyes closed
paws tucked
under his chin

that's not the way to
remember him – recall

him roaring
or running
or leaping, half bear
to catch a ball
bounced off a wall

recall
his heartbeat
as he lay sleeping across me
all six, seven stones of him
the landscape of muscles
beneath his red fur
the power in his neck
his teeth
his eyes
him standing tail wagging
at the bottom of the stairs

recall
the way I felt I
knew him completely
& utterly, even if I
didn't
but the comfort in that
was colossal

as there is none now
in this constant phantom itch
as of a lopped limb
incinerated, ash

my dog my dog
miss him horribly

the fanfare which
was sounding for him inside me
has now
slowed
to a bleak violin
& this
itch
constant, continuous
will never
go away

my dog
my friend you were
I wish you
were still alive
my dog
I wish you
weren't dead

COLM RECOVERING

He lies
on the burst couch
under a thin & crusty
stained duvet,
only his head visible
in the weak morning sunlight,
breath
rattling through
lips whitely scummed
& the fungal runnels of his nostrils,
eyes closed

lashes caked
skin like
uncooked sausage.

A smell comes off him;
sweat & alcohol,
amphetamine & nicotine.
He is a sad bag of spent energy,
a roughly slumbering hump,
gently rising &
softly falling
as he recovers
as he undergoes
the long & loathsome process
again
so he can do it all over
again.

This pathetic pattern
he is lost within.

Look at him;
a waster he is,
a user of hard drugs,
one who gives strong voice
to his desperation
& articulates his joy
in the only way he knows.

What is to be done
with people like this?
Like him?

Well, here he is,
look at him: now
envy him, admire him,
because
two nights ago
among the thumping,
flashing lights and
laughing faces sheened
in sweat he
found, for one
moment in the
chemical cloud,
exactly
what he was looking for,
which maybe you
will never
ever be able
truthfully
to boast.

STRENGTH

infection
or flu
whatever it was
fought off after four days:
Tuesday
I was a lump
groaning and hacking
in a sour puddle
of my own brine
& last night,

Saturday
I was knocking back the beer
& bellowing along
albeit throat-gratingly
to Christy Moore.

No squirmy
little
jumping whiskery
short-arsed little fucker
of a streptococcus
can get the
better of me,
fuck no.

Here it is again; another
crap wee poem-thing
I'll wish to be able to write
when I'm old
& spotted
& fucked,
if
I ever am.

FOR ONCE

Paisley-patterned octopi
wisp & fractal
through the letterbox -
I open the curtains
and am stunned by the light.
Things hover,

about, I believe, to bloom.
I am receiving £70 a week
housing benefit.
I have space & light & time.
Words grow. Are unstoppable.
It's
alright.

FINALLY

They don't all end this way, no,
although it's true they all seem to; with
punches and curses,
real momentary hatred,
tears and teeth gnashing
and hurled crockery
and clenched fists
and the gut-punch of guilt and
revealed betrayal...
this realisation
of waste.

Ah, there were some good things, I suppose;
things to do with
beaches and shells and
alcohol and
laughter
and closeness where there
seemed to be none
and occasional pride,
things concerning
surprise, which are
the most valuable of all.

Well, Jennifer, I may be hating you
at the moment
and equating you with rage
and garbage

but I know
that in this death
can be seen this promise: that
we leave behind us more
much more
than mere
bones.

GOD, WHAT A NIGHT

Maybe it was the alcohol,
the first night sober after several,
or any of the other confusions
which both cause and compound such a session,
or maybe it was watching
Picnic at Hanging Rock
before I went to bed,
or maybe it was pollution,
bewilderment,
just straight terror,

whatever the cause,
last night was a bad one,
populated,
my bedroom seething with them.
Noticed first
when I tried to sleep;

tired,
exhausted,
but the snickering fears
permitted no rest,
and then it was a relief
to awaken,
sheets a sweaty swamp,
falling unconscious
snapped awake
by invisible hands
in the darkness
pulling me out of bed...

restless sleep again
interrupted by a man sobbing.
In the darkness, again,
the sounds of a man sobbing.

Oh yes – they were all there last night,
they all came out,
the whole host
of anxiety and loss.

All I wanted
was to sleep.
Now there's more confusion,
that the manifestations
of dream
are not conducive
to dreaming.
God, I hope I
never succeed.
I hope I die like this;
yearning, longing, and content.

FUCK ALL TO WORRY ABOUT

no nasty letters through the door
no red fuel bills
no eviction notice
no threats of disciplinary action
for non-payment of loans and fines

nothing at all in fact; just a
personal letter for the French girl upstairs,
the address on the envelope
typed in running letters,
which I thought quite interesting

so: 10:20 AM
the radio plays in the bedroom
there is a load of washing
in the machine

I can hear seagulls
the day stretches ahead
waiting to be filled
and I will have no problem in filling it, Christ
I'm only 30 years of age
I have many books to read
letters to write
bouncing ideas waiting to be worded

cottage cheese and tomatoes on toast
tea, coffee
masturbation if I feel like it

the day

will pass the day
will somehow pass
and I will be asleep again
with night outside
the window before
I even
know it

PUS

awful smell rising
from the chest
for several days
a whiff every time I moved
something like
carrion
rot
imagine a green plastic bucket
filled with faeces and spew
left in a warm place
for several weeks

a lump there
just under the skin
between the nipples
it broke open
under my fingertips
and released white matter
that hideous smell elevenfold
in the bathroom
I faced the mirror
squeeeeeeeeeeezed

and in an instant
pus Pollocked the glass
white with a hint of green
stringy, thick, viscous
and the stomach-boiling stench

heaving I stood there
and squeezed til I bled
forced out the reek
squeezing squeezing
the rottenness out

things can't be the same now
I'll go on eating, drinking
breathing, living
knowing that decay
can spread and grow
inside in the secret parts
this vital distillery
boiling brewery
sluicing its waste
out through the skin

in the chamber
where my heart beats
the malign manufactory
makes and matures
what can only be
friendly to death

hangs over my head
black cap, bald patch
hood of pus

KNOWLEDGE

I'd never known the fear & trembling
much less put it into words
but I knew it was on me
as well as I knew
that I was a twenty-year-old boy
reeling back on the bed
smiling
panting under
the happy hammer-blow
of heroin

COCAINE

a bounced cheque
promise unhonoured
a disappointment concomitant
with events diurnal, quotidian,
and beyond all this
a lesson unlearned
guidance ignored

the tap tap tapping of the blade on the mirror
dust into powder
pulverise, pulverise
the face reflected face looming
scoop-eyed, unshaven
sagging at the cheek
and slack at the lip
with a wanting
too strong
to satisfy itself

FINDING

voiceless I was
I would speak
& out would come small sounds
garbage   glossolalia
so I looked
in dustbins
pub toilets
in the barrel of a needle
in women
cells
hospitals
endless grey waiting in government offices
in fists
in the fat faces of policemen
in rooms where the only movement
was the slowly crumbling plaster
in the sea
in the forests
in the mountains

found it eventually
hiding in between
sheets of blank paper
a small voice
squeaking
alone
defenceless but unafraid

here
it is

FREE

Putting the finishing touches
to your PhD thesis
you tap in 'finger'
instead of 'fringe' -
it's understandable, you're tired,
you've been working on this for almost four years -
so you black out the word,
tap delete,
and attempt to tap in the correct word
but you can't
because your index finger is no longer there; there's
no blood, no wound, no glint of bared bone,
simply a smooth stump.
Deletion.
You stare at it and feel no shock,
no fear,
and certainly no pain...
but what there is
is a quick resurgence of interest
in your work, your study,
in your travail played out
on the throbbing green screen,
and with brain fizzing
and heart pounding
you tap in 'thumb',
black it out,
delete.
Your three-pronged hand twitching now
in front of your gulping face.
There's a surge of inspiration
then

and after five minutes
you sit there
before the screen,
mono-fingered,
nipple-less,
nose-less,
lower-lip-less,
minus the bulge on your liver
from too much drinking
in your teenage years,
minus the scar on your chin
from the pointless fist-fight
outside the chip shop in the city
where you did your first degree,
minus the hole in your chest where regret once resided.

You are enjoying this,
and in a torrent of satisfaction,
a sudden surge of creative energy
fulfilled
you tap in 'genitals'
and with a trembling finger
press delete
and immediately
feel a bother
and a yearning
slip away.

You pull out your waistband and risk
a peek; the Action Man you used to dress up
as a child.

The cursor throbs, demands

attention, so, pleased with your new body,
you spell out H-O-P-E,
delete,
and then complete your thesis to perfection.
The photo of you and your scroll
will adorn your parents' mantelpiece; some years later
you will become head of department
in a red-brick
provincial university.
Not in your chosen subject, true,
but it will pay
for plastic surgery.

GOING TO THE PUB WHERE POLLY WILL BE

& the moon & the night & the stars

And Pete is staggering all over the road
among the cars and takeaway cartons
pissed enough for five his size
he says he'll never get over her

going to the pub where Polly will be
& the moon & the night & the stars

slinky shadow of a prowling cat
a huddle in the chippy behind the steamed windows
fat man eating a sloppy kebab
he'll never swim at midnight
in the Gulf of Mexico

going to the pub where Polly will be

& the moon & the night & the stars

chrome afire, burning paint
fallen rainbows in puddles
so many things to shatter and smash
here and not in Hollywood

going to the pub where Polly will be
& the moon & the night the stars

all teeters on a razor's side
soft skin and bones and teeth
eyes bulge in pissy doorways
overcoats hide limp pricks
and perhaps pick-axe handles

going to the pub where Polly will be
Polly will be in the pub

SUSAN AND THE STAIRS

you were at primary school
Belle Vale Juniors
I remember your grin still
and your dark skin
and your bobbed hair
and your dirty white plimsolls
with the toe showing through

you made me laugh
and I wanted to smell you
and sit with you among the buttercups
but I threw

you
down the stairs instead;
only three of them,
by the door in the playground,
I shoved you down them
and you fell
and you cried
and both of us
ran away.

I don't remember your surname
something Irish, I think
and I'm not entirely sure
that your first name was Susan, but
I do remember you,
twenty five years on I do
remember you.

I wonder if you're still there,
in Netherley,
with a pack of kids
and a horrible job
and a husband who repeatedly
throws you down the stairs and worse,
and I wonder if you ever remember
me and those three
concrete stairs,
how it set a pattern
or if it set a pattern
if it was a warning
a foretaste
a premonition
an idea of how memory
can burn and return

and steal sleep
and set your skull to sizzling.

I don't know, Susan,
if that is your name,
what any of this means; I
didn't then, I don't now
and I won't
in times to come.

But I remember you,
you and the stairs; I do, I still
remember
the three grey stairs and you.

MORE DOG DREAMS

and instantly I am bounding leaping
through the snowbound night-time trees
the moon's blue honey
slanting between the dusted branches
snow kicks up around, behind
spring and lope
spring and lope
sprint, leap over
fallen tree-trunks
engine roaring in the chest
muscles bulging with living

there is no cold
or discomfort
only utter exhilaration
aware of movement at the right shoulder

I look
and see you, my dead dog
keeping pace
black leathery lips pulled back in a grin
over wet red slab of a tongue
and in your eyes
black as the sky
my own reflection
I am you
a boxer dog too

we speed up
become
bounding blurs
in the trees

if this is a preview
then I can't wait
if this is a dream then
I thank you, dog
my dead dog
in the trees

WRECKED

and I mean really, genuinely,
truly
this is no good title
this is the real fucking thing
7:43 AM Tuesday morning
I come into the kitchen
for a 2 litre
bottle of wine

ok, glad
of what I did or didn't
do, LFC are out of every-
thing, the moon is rising
over the sea
and my gob is furry
and my dick has shrunk,
shrivelled,
the speed,
y'know,
but all the clouds
are in my throat
and if I swallow
I squeeze out rain,
yes,
this is what the world wants,
God, I am alone, and
happy,
really truly wrecked,
and for now suicide
sits on my face
like a smile, a
promise, a maybe,
maybe only a
maybe.

LIKE THE LUMINOUS GHOSTS

OF BONES IN AN X-RAY

the fall of the white
is directly commensurate
with the severity of the comedown or
hangover; a simple headache after a
few pints with the football produces
only a few floating flakes; and the
crushing collapse, the annihilation,
the hopeless, devastated, eviscerated wreckage
of several days lost in the drugs and the drink
will, if you let it, be swallowed
in a wave of whiteness, unstoppable,
an endless ocean of clean cloud
almost unbearable in its purity.

Well, maybe. Or perhaps it's just one
more
excuse.

WITHOUT FAIL

it's always the same; they
look so cool, they do, the way
they move, the way they laugh,
their stillness with their dark eyes
staring at the invisible, they
don't say much but when they do
it's always perfect, always just the
right thing to say; they roll joints
and sit forward in their chairs,
listening, leaning in to the music,

their lower lip drooping ever so slightly
to reveal just a tiny white glint
of tooth.

That's how it seems. And it
doesn't take long; a month, perhaps,
a month on average, and then there's
agoraphobia, alcoholism, anxiety,
abuse,
a pathological lack of self-confidence
the need to cling
and demand
which of course
means flight
and an exacerbation
of whatever it is that makes them
stare, walk slowly, laugh softly,
their muscles moving beneath their clothes,
their faces wrapped in what seems
to be
a sure and certain sense of themselves. . .

Jesus, how wrong we can be.
How wrong the whole thing is.

REJECTION SLIP

and it fell on me
this hail
and clung
I try to wash it off but it remains
like a scar, vandal grease
it is a love

it is an obsession
I am young and we have
many years together
and when they finally find me
alone and still and blue
in some small and dirty room
they will need to snap my frozen fingers
in order to remove the pen

COUCH

battleship
maroon and bursting
horse-hair innards
shiny steel skeleton
sleeping on it
too drunk to reach the bed
those hours reclining, reading
Rorschach blots of
ink, tea, coffee, sperm, piss, tears
so many nights
the bodies known
tv programmes
battleship
piloting the evenings
courting the doom-beasties
both of us
groaning
armrest a support
for the chin
to view the world
outside
riding the mornings

skating over the afternoons
nap and ticking
arse-familiar
centre of the room
to wall
to window-bay
then diagonal
now perpendicular
mites in you
spiders
ticks in your ticking
burst
watching the sky bleed
orange
red
black
flirting with the whales of wish
the tadpoles of hope
screaming into your cushion
pleading
laughing
back-rest
arm-rest
gorgeous and appropriate names
all those nights
all those days
battleship, battleship
genesis of legion
battleship
carrier of much
battleship
soon there'll be another
to get to know

for me and for you
if you're healed
and that's
all

ONE FOR THE ROAD

when they run me to ground
in my underground lair
and when they gingerly enter
after hearing that last single gunblast
stepping carefully over the bones and booby-traps
they will find on the
walls
ceiling
every little niche
every little furrow
every single inch of masonry and wood
covered
with pictures of you

PILGRIMAGE

Strange how we feel the need   on anniversaries
to re-visit the sites
of past catastrophes

at the extreme
we will seek to climb back inside our mothers
we will spend our lives searching for Eden

today marks 2 years since

since the day we
and I am going back and
I wonder if that place will be drowning in blackness
our drifting shadows still there like the sea behind fog

I wonder if you remember
if you too move through sorrow today
if it powers your limbs and your speech

I will ask the little birds   tomorrow
today   there is a train to catch

FREAKSHOW

Your own granny is the bearded lady &
the three-legged man can be seen
        in any old barroom rapist;
Two-headed Janus smiles & sneers
        in each & every big or little lie.
This here is the real thing:
    meet the baby-man,
still wears nappies & suckles milk from his mama,
his age the same as the size of her titties;
a real broken heart in a reinforced glass case,
torn still warm & cleft neatly in two
from the hanging breast of a suicide;
Billy Two-beards Two-noses, the auto-fellatio man;
the man brought up by a family of newts,
found behind his own desk in an
        accountancy firm;
they're all here, & more;
the Fat Lady, so obese she has to be

kept away from airports due to her geo-
     magnetic orbit;
he who weeps constantly & sits in a bath
full of his own salty tears;
the boy who eats dung;
the two lovers who never met;
the Siamese Twins, boy & girl,
 joined – guess where – at the groin;
Mrs. Owl, the lady who can move her head
 through 360°; learned, she says,
     through fear;
Mr. & Mrs. Woof, man & dog & husband &
wife, see love transcend all specie.
These - & more – will open your eyes.
Children not allowed.
Entrance £1.50.
Concessions for the old & unemployed.

WHY? WELL, LISTEN

because you can't fucking fly
because you can't swim
  you can't swim like seals can swim
because you can't cope with the fact that
  somewhere there are four tons of TNT
  aimed directly at you
  & another four tons
  for each person you might love
because you don't understand icebergs
    or dogs
    or signal fires
    in the desert
because you are entranced by the labels

        on jars of jam in the supermarket
because you can't sleep
because you really can't fly
because you would like to dream in colour both
                    asleep &
                    awake
because your larynx is useless
& you would love to be able
      to sing like the whales
because the taps drip
because there is never enough money
because of mould
    & mildew
       & endless dishes of pasta or rice
because of menstruation
because of the way you stand motionless
            at your window
            to watch the birds
because of the way you love your children
because of the guns
   & the tanks
   & the scattered limbs
   & the graves
& because you really, really, truly, cannot fucking fly

RAM THE TREE UP THE ANGEL'S ARSE

doing all this over someone else
is not like doing it over you
and that will make this -
    Christmas, 1993 -
      my twenty seventh -
OK   pigeons, not knowing

will bow puff-chested on every promenade
and eat rich pickings if they're lucky
unlike the turkeys. Like always, still
there will be terror in many faces
but I will be looking to new legs and
laughter and a presence soon to be probably
permanent   if only for a short time

you may chip your tooth on the sixpence
in this poem and then you can cultivate
a cute and dissolute grin
you may find that the wishbone will scream
when snapped – that the Christmas crackers
will contain messages that inform you
of the exact time and manner
of your death
            or that the beautifully wrapped
presents beneath the dying tree contain
severed human limbs, meticulously cleaned
and twinkling

maybe this year will be ours
I hardly know you, you're new   but
on the morning of the fifth day from now
there will be smiles and hangovers, delight
and disappointment, no snow

Hitler   Thatcher   Jeffrey Dahmer
were all, all children once, sleeping and dreaming
of flying to the moon

STONED

snowflakes on central heating
        refrigerator thrum

these words
blitzed
trashed
fucked
wasted
cabbaged
faced
garbaged
hammered
wrecked
smashed
battered

floating father, feathery flower
        through a rent in the sky bring
armageddon and honey

EVERYTHING IS CLEAN

put all insecurities in the washing machine
all uncomfortable discoveries
        on heavy soil cycle
drink coffee and smoke
and how could she let the fat pornographer
            inside her
I don't know that I don't know
might as well measure the curlicues
            of a whelk

in terms of time
should I read the letters
ask the black fat vulture grinning
      in that future
everything is clean
everything is nice
nothing is murdered or mutilated or dying
    or irreparably fucked up

COITUS INTERRUPTUS

I dunno, maybe,
what would the cats do?

This summer wind makes a furnace world
and my friend has caught me wanking
and my belly burns as if of acid I
had drunk
and the woman walking naked through the
kitchen
today does not soften what I smash my
        face against the brick wall of
            this life

in the outhouse I'd do it
with the webs and wet walls
and the sneering spiders
and the beams where I once
saw a roosting bat

WAVING A CAN OF STOUT

LIKE A BLACK FLAG OF TRUCE

whatever they are
those reeking reasons
whatever past spillage
causes such stains to spread
the scum-spume of which
are manifest
in these objectionable actions
I can cope with them all tonight

tonight
the spiders can swing and suck
tonight
the shylocks can wring their palms
tonight
the tarot will all fall into place
and if I feel   ah fuck it
the pressures of these nuisances
I will simply sit
pounce-less
and let them hang in the air
and watch them not rot
watch them never fester

whatever they are
this orbiting awfulness
they can run wild tonight
they can destroy everything
they can rub their stink off
on all around
they can spread their pus
and boils and rashes

they can murder and mutilate
everything forever
tonight if
they
want to.

MORNING SUNLIGHT, COLOUR OF CIDER

when your partner is asleep
when you're hungover
when the twats who live upstairs
are playing bad music far too fucking loud
when all you can taste is stale tobacco
when you've just found in your kitchen
a bag of black mush that once was carrots
when you've got no cat to admire
and your balls are boiling
the best you can settle for is this:

some toothpaste
a notebook and a pen
cold water on the face
coffee
and a retreat into the cavern that has
your name on the door

HELICOPTER

buzzes all morning
      overfed wasp
takes pictures
      which now hang on a notice-board
      in the police station
my house circled in red ink

awful bloated wasp
were I in you
the view I know
would be beautiful

I don't know what the words are for this
      I truly don't

VISITATION

the water in the toilet bowl
is rippling in the wind

rain

on the radio: John Smith, Labour party
leader, has died of a massive heart attack

rain

real coffee, tobacco, books and a ceiling
are all you really need, although
other things
may add a bit of spice -

floating around the kitchen, turning

somersaults, bouncing safely off all six sides;
fellatio;
vitamin pills, talismanic, tiny lilac
eggs of some minute and mythical bird;
spring water in the fridge;
a tame raccoon nesting in the airing cupboard;
a battered tomcat, dirty white,
stalking across the floor towards you,
blue eyes (his, not yours) on fire

rain

a smiling old woman
to stroke my face and tell me that
everything is going to be okay

rain

still, the water in the toilet bowl
is rippling gently in the wind

AFTER SHAVING

harvested stubble
iron filings out
into the far, far
places of water

twinkling water
refrigerator hum
rasp of the razor
and this is all

shaving in silence

baring the face
chin freckled
with spots of blood

demented Santa Claus
God-like sees all
wriggles down your chimney
to leave rotting fruit at your bedside

and stand over you
masturbating
while you
sleep

raw skin
spotted, impure
blood drips
blood drips

my cells now in Cardigan Bay
only gentle radiation
this motion, this watching
this making clean

drone of an aeroplane
over the hill
my face is my own
and stays the same to me

nick and slice
the head of a zit
tiny pink cap
tiny volcano

here is no mystery

here are no tygers
only this routine baptism
oh you lucky fucking fishes

MOULD

the old man in the fishmonger's
held the herring head-high
and said:

" that eyes remind me of rats
   means that
tonight my poor paella -
   no, my kedgeree -
will taste of rust
   and every thrush in the district
will forget how to sing
   and mother
take me away
come and save me
razors are nothing but cold steel
rats are nothing more than
   essential".

You're not wrong, feller, I
said, and bought a handful
of prawns.

SUICIDE NOTE

you step out of the bath
and dry yourself with a damp towel
without set or symmetry;
only one leg and only one arm
(on opposite sides)
forget your lower back,
your arse,
your hair,
forget to clean your ears
or deodorise your armpits. . .
you get confused.
Christ how you get confused

you've got a specific tableau
all ready to use
as your last thought;
a face, a voice
some smell-memory,
certain lighting,
a touch, maybe,
emotion recollected
in cataclysm

you turn the central heating off
defrost the fridge
leave a note for the milkman,
cancelling all deliveries

LIVERPOOL 8, 4AM

oily rain
taps at the window
as a distant dog
barks at a passing siren
& the car alarm
which began to shriek
when I went to bed
3 hours ago
finally
stills, & is
quiet. I am
privileged.

WONDERING WHO I'D BE IF I WASN'T BORN ME

This is me waking up;
see how I stare for a minute or two
before I
move.

This is me eating; raising toast
and mug
to my mouth in mechanical movements
and looking out the window
at whatever passes by.

This is me at toilet, laughing
over an old copy of *Viz*
while guts strain and push.

Here is me reading.
Here is me scratching

insect bites on
my arms and legs.

Look at me praying silently, seeking
to open negotiations with whatever
I feel to seethe and weep
in the low clouds.

This is me cooking, mixing
strong flavours.

This is me lifting weights,
sweating, teeth gritted and eyes
screwed up
enjoying myself
kind of.

Now here is me
watching television, faces
at my shoulder.

This is me stroking a cat.

This is me smoking.

This is me waiting,
forever waiting, teeth
clicking very softly in
light moon and sodium, soap suds
drying in my ears
from the shower you haven't seen
me take.

Now here is me sleeping, a state
I've never been able to see myself

in, before.

A DREAM

The city is four vast bridges,
spanning a colossal valley,
linked by many smaller bridges,
tightropes, chairlifts, ladders, webs
of hairy rope, complex pulley-systems...
Buildings cling to the girders like barnacles
or sprout from stanchions
or hang on hawsers beneath,
clustered like hemorrhoids
above the river
thousands of feet below.
People teem and seethe and scurry,
darting like mice,
flitting from bridge to bridge like spiders
or crippled birds, pulling themselves
up the girders and down the girders
like hybrids of ape and aphid.
It is all incessant movement,
granite, sandstone, red tile
and sooty steel.

I sit in a pub drinking black beer
and looking out on this mad city
through a greasy window which
advertises a brand of whisky
I've never heard of and can't remember.
I am waiting for Deborah.
When she arrives, when she appears
out of the fevered dripping web,

we are going to get drunk
and go to the flat-roofed club
which hangs on cables
beneath the middle bridge
and can only be reached by a cage
operated by men in uniforms
with peaked caps and golden frilled epaulettes.
First, though, I need to be clean,
and I know there are showers
upstairs in the pub for public use,
so I ask the barman (plump,
walrus moustache, red face)
if I can use one and he
points to the ceiling and I
climb spiral stone stairs,
dank and dripping but smelling
of soap and freshness.
I come out into a well-lit
yellow landing and hear water pattering
and see a vague naked shape
behind a steamed-up frosted-glass door.
The shape puts its head round the door,
wet hair helmet, shouts 'hiya!'.
It is Deborah. We greet and kiss
and while she completes her shower
I decide to shit and go through a
door marked 'toilet' into a long, long
corridor with a cubicle at the end,
thimble-sized at this distance.
I walk towards it. It is full of
someone else's crap, stained orange
tissue. I flush it away, sit,
shit, wipe, flush again, then
go back down the corridor and have, while

Deborah dresses, a wonderful,
completely cleansing shower
which leaves me
smelling of honey-suckle.
I dress in my coolest clothes,
put a crucifix around my neck,
put my hand on my hip
and make a triangle of my elbow
which she threads her arm through
and linked like that
we descend the stairs
and go out into that crazy, heaving,
hanging, impossible
and welcoming place.

LIVERPOOL 5, KOSICE 0

A gnat   flits
across the television screen,
casting a shadow
      on the green
which
like a pterodactyl
through the legs of a brontosaur
figure-of-eights
around Robbie Fowler's legs,
well recovered now
from their
      cruciate ligament
injury

ANIMALS

we must appear to them
as oncoming balls of devouring flame
as
small stains above
which explode and spread
and turn the sky to ink

we must stink
so bad to them
that the insides of their skulls
burn
and roar

the sound of our footsteps
the rustle of plastic
as we move towards them in blackness
must
turn their hearts to tumbling ice
and turn
their warm blood to ooze

our cleanliness
is their terror
our cures
their wars
children skinless and screaming
in napalm
or phosphorous
or plague

we make them reach to us
through bars
and blind them and cripple them and rob them

of speech
so that they cannot tell us what we already know -
that we love
to murder ourselves

that we look forward eagerly
to raping our babies

that we adore wallowing
in quags of our own making

that we eat our own shit
with relish

say they made a religion
how does it feel to be Satan

TRAINING POOL FOR INJURED SWANS

Some swim, lopsided
some stand, ungainly
some hobble to the water's edge
then hobble back again.

Some flap one wing and some one stump,
some flap two stumps,
some stand on one leg
and stare one-eyed.
Count the variable equations
of mutilation.

Some were found broken at the
feet of weirs.
Some were found propeller-hacked,

red lightning across their wings and breasts.
Some were discovered
at the edges of canals
or city ponds,
among the plastic, among the tin,
wrapped in nylon or oily rope.

Some were found
shot through with bolts or bullets,
others
wobbling under mercury,
metal swallowed in weight form
or water form, leeched
into the rivers
by the factories nearby.

Count the equations,
always variable, of
mutilation.

Now they cough and limp and stagger
and fall, trying
to reach the water
or the sky; their
healed stumps take them
only into the mud.

Approach them, they will
hiss,
telling you
what you already know, or
suspect – what hope
could there be for such falling grace.

What stupid providence
would let them
create themselves so, their great wings
to be stolen, their
whiteness to be sullied, their
eyes to be seared atop
their question-mark
virgin necks.

SCABIES

Covered in sticky Dercon cream
I try to feel them
writhing in their burrows, dying
leaving me alone. No more
nights thrashing at my flesh.
No more scratching
until I bleed. No more
hosting these nasty little
miracles, small burrowers, wee
wondrous subcutaneous horrors
setting up home
in my skin to erupt it in minute
red volcanoes, you tiny marvels, I
sit here sticky
and can't bathe for 15 hours, micro-
scopic magical invisible riddles, you
horrible little fuckers, die,
die, die.

THE MERSEY IN MY VEINS

the same fluid

moves through me
as reflects the Liverpool lights;
maybe that's why
I too
can sometimes smell
of shite

HACKLES

we were about nineteen
or twenty

we were drunk
it was 2AM

and we vaulted the fence
into Chester zoo

and stopped being boys
and became
shapes

leaping like gibbons
skulking like lynxes
eyes darting like those
of birds
or antelopes

an owl hooted
somewhere
something cackled
and the smells

were of
rotting fruit and vegetables
musk
earth
blood
sweat
the rank breath of carnivores

something moved
beside me
it drifted through the moonlight
slow, low
hulking
hairy
huge but
hugging the ground

its flank
rippled through a moonbeam

I
caught sight
of a leg muscle
cartwheel-sized
resilient

piston-powerful

I heard mucus rattle
as I was
sniffed and assessed

and felt
threat
creep up my back
loosen my sphincter
tense my legs
into coiled
springs

a bird
screeched

moon fell
bluely
and a roar
in the blackness
had us leaping
the chain fence
in giggling terror

screaming away in the car
as jubilant
and relieved
and horrified
as any first-time
escapee

GET IN, GET OUT, STOP FUCKING ABOUT

because
the grave-eagle

has its talons in your hair
so if you must
waste a day
smoking
wanking
staring at the tv
then at least
make sure
that you hate
it

WET DREAM AT 32

waking up

that sweet
sperm smell

late October morning
cold
very bright

still sea

that muscular brown woman
in towering heels

taking control

feel as if
I've been
plunged somewhere
incredibly

deep

vastly
comforting

slight snarl
on the thickly lipsticked
mouth

that sweet
sperm smell

this is how I grow my garden
just look
at my pretty flowers

NO QUESTIONS ASKED

the road will unspool &
the car bonnet
will lead us
through greasy windscreen rain-diamonds

our clothes will be comfortable
when we buy the gun

large birds will take off
from behind the houses

clouds will gather & open

the papers will clarion our names
the television

will buckle under the wrongness of us
there will be scared
running

our hearts will beat faster

we will kiss in carnage

& use money
as our raft

we will drink the river
put the mountains in
our rucksacks

let multi-coloured light
rainbow our faces
as we stare out at the sky
through stained glass

because
it will be sunny
the light throbbing in our wings

when we buy
the gun

COMING UP TO ARMISTICE DAY, 1998

80 years on
and they wear ties

to tell the camera
of that vast
godless botch

of that mistake
drenched in mud
and memory

of piling the brains
back into the
shattered skulls of friends

they have taken
the trenches
into their faces
and now
they wear them like medals

death dodged
decades ago
the bullets beaten
the ousted shells

they still talk of immense luck
as the shadow
unfurls from the ground

put down the bottle
don't need the needle
these
have seen everything
you've ever hoped or dreaded
these have done more
than you'll ever think of doing

these lives
will rust your dreams
corrode all your wild adventures

and still
they crouch
under bombardment

age's reek

undefeatable they are they
cracked the earth and
the planet span
under their tramping feet

still
carrying their carnage
with them
as they sink into mist

they remind us
that
we will never see
them again

when

we have not seen
them yet
THIS JUST IN

an island
has been discovered

between Scotland & Iceland
a large chunk
of volcanic rock
with some vegetation
& meager strips
of fertile soil. A
modern-day, more gruesome
Marie Celeste type mystery,
it appears that all adults
over 18
have fled, & all children
& infants
have been crucified
on the house doors
of the island's
only
one-street village.
They have been dead
for little more than
a month.
One child
was wearing a crown of thorns
another
had a pentagram
carved into her chest
others have been
similarly
disfigured.
What went on here
we shall never know; what
became of the adults
we shall never know.
This simple lump
of sea-blasted rock

has been called
First-Island Island, and it
belongs to no-one
but the indigenous
rats
and well-fed gulls.
Tourist trips
to there
are to begin tomorrow; see
your local travel agent
for details.

INSOMNIA

alcohol withdrawal maybe
but the faces
float from the fog
when you close your eyes
& the whispering
in the darkness begins   things
flapping
around your bed   your head
you wait
for the creak & heavy movement
of something
climbing into bed
beside you
for the rattle of the window
being raised in its frame
for the kick of smoke
from the still-lit
cigarette end

in the bin

your heart thuds
as you remember times
of arrogance & coldness
ridiculous posturing
words spat
faces shoved & all
energy spent
wrongly   you think that
for all these things
there will come a time
when you must pay
& that
this night is it

you
curl tightly
into yourself
& think of
snowbound forests
desert islands
warm shelter in a snowstorm
a scenario
in which you act
heroically   then you
scratch the back of your leg
fiercely
& are terrified
at the sound of your own voice
saying something about
forgiveness for my sins
forgiveness for my life   just
please

let me sleep

ALL GROWN UP

I can bathe
with a bottle of cold Martini
& some favourite music, I
can sing
& admire my own muscles
as I make myself
smell good
& dress in my favourite clothes.
I can listen
to more music
on my own
in my own space
as I drink more Martini
& snort amphetamine
off the coffee table.

I can make myself
feel
utterly invincible.

& I can make
my buzzing way
to the pub
at the appointed time
to meet
my grown up friends,
hunched up
against the cold,
walking in the road

to avoid falling
icicles & slates
from the gutters of the secret houses,
trying not to attract
the attentions of the listening
policeman
or catch the eye of the too-loud
shouter in the bar.

I can
talk to women
of jobs & origins
& favourite films,
I can drink too much
& spew up
in the pub toilets
or down a damp alleyway
or even in the sea.

I can do
anything.

I can hurt myself
if that's what it takes
to banish
the sudden-swooping spread shadows,
to drown out
the shrieking in my ear
or still the trembling in my legs.
I can
awake
wanting to pray for death,
my face swollen & blood
in my shit,

all my money gone
& my clothes torn & befouled.

I can
wonder how I got here,
& how I can go away again; I
can laugh
at bosses, fat controllers,
make myself ill
on the nectar
of my breakout.

I can do
anything, I'm an adult; I'm
all grown up
now.

OPEN ALL HOURS

We would thieve
& sell
anything; books, clothes, cameras,
drugs, a typewriter, this
stuff of our earlier lives
converted gratefully
& frantically, working
the miracle
of that first drink & the
loosening of all tension
as our blood flowered
into dilution.

It was gorgeous & terrible,

just the two of us & our
thirst & our wrongness
in the corner
by the pool-table,
that dark corner,
we would drink away
all drink-guilt
& enforced vileness, all
the humiliation & shame
of being alive, here,
then.

No sleep, at 9 AM
we'd be persuading the Spar staff
to sell us wine; at 10 AM
we'd be sitting on the castle battlements
drinking the dregs & staring
out to sea; & at 11 AM
we'd be in the pub, that
dark corner, the day to be blurred away
crossing snow-bound bridges
& vomiting in toilets
& returning, always returning
to the chapel
of each other's presence
on the seat,
behind the table,
in that dark corner.

We would sell anything
for that. We would thieve
anything for that.

& on such stuff

we have built ourselves, foundations
soft as beer-froth, never slippery,
never elusive, because it is always
there. We
planted a seed in it, didn't we?
& it
will grow.

THREE WISHES

a dark sky
over a dark sea
behind a dark beach
some large clouds
sun-rimmed
near low islands
topped by fire
rocks
some young seals
flopping towards the breakers
like giant slugs
wheeling birds calling lonely
bayonets of marram
shuddering in the sharp wind
volcanic cinders and black sand
and giant blobs of clean rain
ricocheting off the window
of the small stone cottage
illuminated by a driftwood fire
and heated by whisky
and bubbling stew,
no visitors

only the birds and the seals
and the long wands
of flourishing sunlight
dull-golden across the salt water
and I don't need
the other two

SMUDGED

I can do this now,
talk about
the way
you wouldn't go,
the way
your small-tiger paws
had thinned
to sinewy coarse-fur twigs and
still you wouldn't go,
the way
the sleek and prowling muscles
of your flanks
had warped and twisted and
bulged with tumours and
still you wouldn't go,
the way
your eyes had faded
and your teeth
had fallen out
and your lashing tail
had decayed
and your claws
had become dislodged and

still you wouldn't go,
the way you fought and turned
on the needle,
small cat old cat
needing enough drug
to fell a big dog.

Praying for you to go and
still you wouldn't
go.

All those years, you
greeting me,
sleeping on me,
bringing me torn
birds and starfish,
once a whole roast chicken,
all ways to
ascertain
that the patch of tabby colouring
inside me
would never fade.

You
old cat,
spitting at death,
you great old cat,
hissing
at the stupidity
which imprisons
a burning and a whirlwind
in a sad sack
of a moving shell.

Slowly decaying,
decreasing
as the tumour grew
from golfball to
orange to
grapefruit.
Dying slowly as I
prayed for you to go
and you showed me
that the way to go
is to refuse to go,
to spit sparks and glare
and blare until the very end,
until I am smothered in soil,
to kick away
all ageing and loss
and slow deceleration
and to consistently and with real need
pray for things to happen,
even though I know
that they won't.
There will be more.

SOME REASONS

I'll take the football
on a Sunday afternoon,
the quarter-final,

curtains closed to block
out the world & anything
not-football,
the beer in the fridge,
yes,
I'll take the girlfriend
asleep on the couch
& the dying day behind the drapes,
the rapture at the goals,
lifting, rising,
I'll accept this poor perfection, this
splendid substitute,
close the curtains
& turn on the TV
& open the can
& light a cigarette
& just for two hours
want or wish
for nothing, no,
just for the day to die
the result to go my way
& the girlfriend to
wake up.

HOMEWARDS

I imagine
a meeting in a cobbled street
a bright city morning

horse-dung in steaming lumps
gold-tipped canes
& top hats & spats
& frock coats & frame dresses with
the woman gliding beneath

barefoot mucky urchins
asking for pennies
an old man flat-capped
on the corner outside the inn
hawking newspapers
telling of some far-off, escalating
war

this is easy to remember

so many things
are so easy to recall
without a sense of loss

like the human heart
removed & bleeding
on an icy white slab
alone
in an abandoned warehouse,
just that

HIGHER POWER

the man stands trembling
up there
he's in a bad way
he tells us his name

and that he's an alcoholic

smoke curls into ampersands
parentheses and question-marks

he tells of
nights lost   of days squandered
of possessions taken away
of a woman badly
beaten
of being refused entry to the hospital
ward
of losing his teeth
of shit
running down his trouser legs
of things too vile
too unforgiveable -
he can't talk about them yet
in public

maybe that will come, that
confidence, that self-forgiveness
that acceptance of
powerlessness – it's
come to thousands before
and it will come to thousands after

there are groans of recognition at his
words
nods, murmurs

his knees are
trembling, nerves
or DT's

what teeth remain
gleam yellow
in the halogen

his face hangs
off his bones
like it wants to leave his head
it's had
enough

and so has he – he
makes way
for another steersman
on this tragic fucking adventure
that none of us
ever asked
for

BECAUSE IF YOU'RE ALREADY HORIZONTAL, NO-ONE CAN KNOCK YOU DOWN

summer comes over the waves
like soaring birds of silver
reminding us
of the times
we've had money
& brings with it news
of bombs
& a war creeping closer

young women wear less
every day

& a child's skull
catches a nail

whole families
become mangled twisted
heaps of burst flesh
& the sun shines

Wales & Scotland
will have their own parliaments
& the mountains won't fall
the seas won't dry
the bats won't find
a new way to track their prey
& the icebergs
won't crack yet

mathematics will always be boring
& ice-cold vodka
will always taste
like the purr of a cat

the moon won't slip
& the earth won't shift
but maybe anyway
we should all just go to bed

yes
maybe we should all just stop what we're doing
just lay our heads down
& sleep

DREAMLESSLY

this promise
in the rain-gutted sky: that
there will come a day
when
you will be taken out of an airport concourse
by a kindly man
& led towards an unmarked door
behind which
will be
your parents, in tears, &
behind them, a
policeman, &
behind the policeman, a
priest

BREAKING THROUGH

In a Liverpool pub
some years ago
the television
showed the Berlin wall
being smashed to pieces.
An old man
shook his head sadly
and said: Fucking vandals.
Disgusting. Should
all be taken out
and shot.

HILLSBOROUGH

Colm can't
move.

Someone is shaking him
& telling him that his ma
is on the phone
but he
can't
move.

He knows he is in Tuebrook
somewhere
lying on a mattress
in his own puke

& he knows that
he was supposed
to catch the train to Sheffield
earlier

but that's all.

The girl
with the scarred wrists
is telling him
that
lots of people are dead
there are many people dead
there is a field
on the other side of the country
covered with the dead

but Colm
can't
move.

He wants to speak to his mother
he is uncomfortable
lying there
in this strange house

with old sick
cold on
his skin

but
all he can do
is fail to
move.

HALLOWEEN, 1997

another grandmother
dead
& maybe as our eyes close
we see them all, the
remembered ones, welcoming
us, greeting us, & maybe
that's why we say
their names
as our brains shut down
& our hearts
stop

maybe
that's the point of it all
that gathering
as the light fades
& maybe
that's what we strive for
from the moment of birth -
the red splashes
in the shouting room – that desire
to meet again
& join
& touch
the place where we will all sing
together &

maybe
this will be made
bearable

mother
hold me I'm
trembling

GETTING READY TO GO OUT

What a difference a night can make; who
knows what happened, maybe
the blessings prayed for
have been granted, the

Halloween night
opened like a curtain & let in
not ghosts
but glee; ah, acceptance
can take two forms – sad & angry resignation
with wet eyes &
gnashing of teeth or
this:

drink hard, fuck deeply,
eat, sleep, & laugh, because
tomorrow will come & no cunt will be able
to take it away from
you.

NECESSITY

Maternal granny sends small boy
to the shop
for bara
 to eat with the cawl.
Tell him I'll be in to pay him next week.

Paternal granny sends small boy
to the shop
 to get some aran on tick
 to fry with the druisheen.
Ach, he's not going to resist your wee face .

Two words, same thing; but when
he reaches the shop the boy
knew exactly

what to ask for.

CAN YOU IMAGINE HOW HOT IT WAS, TO MAKE THAT PLACE SEEM COLD?

Manic gurning fucker

here it
comes

the rain on the window
a hail of suicidal insects

faces gulped &
ablaze in
light

gurning in your eyeballs
jaw clenched
as if in pain

sweat heaving
never ending

but
the waiting is too long
although when it comes
it's
rarely disappointing

how long or
how soon

dig
to find means
to alleviate
this wait

maniac gurning foolish

two tatterdemalions
tossed
in burning
darkness

there it goes

wish
for it to stay
for it to
never go away

wish
it would come
back

DISHWASHER

Nearly midnight &
nothing moves, nothing
is reflected in the
gleaming chrome surfaces

& glistening sinks,
knives hanging in racks of
terrible teeth & my ears
ring as I lean back
against the shining
steel basin & eat
leftover potatoes, listening
to the sudden happy chirrup
of the Insect-o-cutor
as it blasts away another one
foolish enough to be drawn
towards its lethal
lilac lightning.

YOU DON'T ALWAYS HAVE TO TRY IT TO KNOW YOU WON'T LIKE IT

Whose van this is &
which mountains these are
I don't know, but I wake
up in both of them.

Me inside one inside the other,
freezing with cold and hangover,
suddenly awake in the passenger seat &
gulping air made syrupy
with petrol & last night's sweated Scotch.

I take deep breaths of this air
& sit in the silence; just some birds
& some wind buffeting the van.
I clear a hole with my sleeve
in the condensation on the window
& see on one side

a small row of stone cottages,
curtains drawn, whitewashed, & on the other
the immense humps of mountains.
A vast green toast-rack.

I feel my body for injuries & find none.

Some cars hiss past; unknown people
on their way to work.

Hungry, I open the glove-box
& find
some empty crisp packets,
a half full box of Bensons,
a Stanley knife
& some hand-written receipts
for stuff like paint & nails
& wood.
Take the cigarettes
& get out, spew in the grass
at the side of the road
as the shivering intensifies.

I don't know where
I am. I
light one of the Bensons
but throw it away half smoked,
start walking with
my thumb out hoping
for a stranger to stop &
take me home.

NEVER WEAR WHITE BOXER SHORTS ON A SIX DAY DRINKING BINGE

when things gradually become
merely black & white
like a Murdoch newspaper
or a zebra's hide

to hide in public houses away
from the first few days
of 1998

oh the shapes we twist each other
into – I drink lager with vodka chasers
& can only think of
policemen
& what they do with the people they've arrested
Christ hammered to the cross
soldiers
in a war
the awful acrobatics
of hard-core porn

the New Year city throbs outside
slippery with brain
grey with rain
from a sky of sand-blasted glass

I raise one cheek
but
decide against it – sooner the retention
of poison gas
than the horror of revealing

streaky underwear later, my
lover watching
from the bed

too much activity
in the putrid brewery
too much ingestion
of angry bubbles

cowering in a pub in the port
drinking away a hangover
wearing underwear which
later
when crumpled on a lino floor
in a moon-blue room might
look like
a discarded wedding veil
ribboned with dark blood

MY FRIEND RAT

If you must love, then
love
these beady eyes, these
blackberry eyes seed-round
seed-shiny, caress
these tiny muscles
& admire these
tiny claws. See
in this scaly cable tail
an evolutionary wonder; hear
in these secret scratchings

the small animal trust, the
growing movement towards
you.

All this can spread outwards, ever-
reaching, until you
too
feel the pain of the needle
in the tumoured belly,
the labouring of the little heart
in the anaesthetic overdose.
And you will offer your
hand for the
little life to die in, &
feel in your chest
the loss of it, the
ending of it, the
awful hole of its absence.
I remember him
sitting on my shoulder.
I remember him sleeping
under my chin.
Rat, I miss you.

AWE

A three-month long barrenness
missing inspiration

now
at midday
 April 5th,
1998
manifests itself as an image
 of a 17th century northern city
preparing itself
for nuclear attack
&
as people scurry
for cellars
& holes
in stovepipe hats
breeches
billowing skirts
buckled shoes
a siren howling
a shadow darkening everything
I imagine
their terror
& don't know
why

OLD MAN IN SEARCH OF DISCARDED PONOGRAPHY

under squealing sea-
gulls, crab-picking across landfill,

dodging bulldozers & sharp spikes of
metal imagine
the thrill of triumph &
fulfilment when you spot the
vagina flapping in the wind
between lung-like plastic bottles
& broken toasters

GORGEOUS

red wine hangover
red wine shite
treacle marmite
fingers break through the paper
sink into mush
& in the mirror above the sink
I see the eyes in blue bags
grease-clogged hair pulled over a bald patch
cracked lips
peanut butter caught in the stubble
raw meat skin
yellowing teeth dulling a grin
snot
dry flakes on cheeks and nose
breath like a hoover bag
stalactites of wax in the ears O
lovely gorgeous
me

WHEN IT COMES

it can crash in your ears
like a thousand seventh waves

the tv gurgling at your back
2 AM with the rain outside
dousing the town and you are
falling in love with the postman
and chilled grapefruit juice

your fridge boils with contraband
coffee and eggs on the other side of
star-dark and a journey through mountains
and a new life, baby boy, small

cat curled asleep on the couch
one eye stitched closed with blue cotton
and the lamplight silhouettes your head
on the wall with your shaggy hair

and the cat's tail twitches and it just
comes and comes and comes

TARIFF

D'yeh know, she said, removing
my knob from her gob,
that it would cost anybody else
30 quid for me to do this to them?

I know, I said.

AND I'd make them wear a rubber, she said.

Then
warmth.
Then

wetness.

I'm glad, I said.

CELL

Along the bare corridor
each heavy riveted door of steel
bears its pair of shoes, parody of
the posh hotel and the polisher; scuffed
and collapsing army boots, leather
worn down to grey, burst
trainers, seam-split, laces
trailing like tentacles.
Mine join them and I am slammed
in.
Four walls, yellow; steel door; concrete
floor; stainless steel toilet with a shoal
of fag-ends and a peep-hole; wooden bed
with two thin rubber mattresses and
nothing else; nothing to look at, no
dialogue to steal, no words to
pluck out of this snared air. When
I have gnawed all my nails
down to blood and
picked my nose completely clean of
snot, I make pellets
out of the toilet roll and flick
them at the pan. No
sound. Twenty straight hits
and I won't be charged. No
sound. I clench my bladder,

trying to squeeze out urine,
just for something to do because
pissing is movement, is
motion. No rivers here. No
sound. FUCK   TH gouged
in the grey paint
on the door. A window made
up of sixty small squares
of span-thick, murky
glass. No breeze. I
take my socks off and pick my toenails
and will go on doing this until
they let me out.

SURRENDERING

Beige fortress on the Parc-y-llyn road
& I stop outside the police station
bail form in the pocket
to watch the bats snatch moths
from the street-light's halo.
Almost too quick for the eye to follow
they wheel and dart in high-pitched chitter,
are snapped into the amber glow & then
yanked back again with the jerk of
life's elastic, flickering between the stars.
Accusation, arraignment, maybe
another cell awaits, beige fortress on the road
to Parc-y-llyn, but I can stretch and pull
these seconds out long as sonar bounces
off my skull and the street-lights' glow is
strobed by these free and frantic, swooping things.

NEVERTHELESS

and
we all
want it to rain

like an expression of grudging gratitude
on Christmas morning
for a shirt
when what you really wanted
was a tenner

we all sit here praying
for it
to rain

IN A FIELD IN SAUGHALL MASSIE

We thought we had it then, didn't we,
on our backs in the long grass or
the dunes,
the acid and the booze and the boots and the
women,
with the small flying insects
coming out of the clouds
and hopping over the waves.

And maybe we did; the talk from Lincoln
to Wales bounced off Merseyside now
concerns break-ups and babies,
big things, not frogs or photographs,
filling the spaces between us with

hugeness.

And maybe we have it still,
maybe
we have it all
yes
we have it all -
the soaring with the owl -
knowing now that we can't twist time,
that all the years they give us
will forever remain
like sand that once was rock.

ACCEPTANCE

Their eyes, mouths, the
whole downward slant of their faces:
You? You've written a novel
which is getting published? By
a big company? YOU? Christ,
I've seen you puking
pathetically in pubs, fighting with the bouncers,
trying it on with women who want
fuck all to do with you, I've
seen you shambling down the prom
on a Sunday morning with sick
down your shirt and piss stains on
your jeans, Christ, how could YOU
have written a novel?

This is there, in them,
all of this, I
see it and I know it's there

and I don't know why and nor do I care
which
is what this whole thing is about,
isn't it, cunt.

JUST FEEL HOW MY HEART IS BEATING

drunken night, three bottles in and
the talk gets round to sex, as it
usually, sometimes, occasionally does – well,
not the sex itself but those
we'd had it with, and we
stripped them down again
into simple details; the one with the piercings,
the tattooed one,
the pregnant one, the black
one, Chinese, the one with the
shaved
head, the one with hair to her arse,
the spotty one, the
sad one, the divorced one, the widowed
one, the students, the nurses,
the daughters, the wives, the
mothers...

& I fell into a laughing blackness
remembering, remembering,
the tang of salt on skin
& the talk of weather & ice-cream &
families & photographs
with their faces pressed to the painted wood
of bed-side tables & how
featureless our talk then seemed, facile &

irredeemable, maybe even cruel, we
drank the whiskey & blethered the night
away & my memories were torn &
abused & discarded.

So maybe I *should* sleep
with that fat bird. Her with the
hairy nose-wart.

STRONG LEGS

God she had such strong legs

they were developed
through riding horses
dancing
trampolining

the thigh-muscles stood out
like cables
hard to the touch

and the calf-muscles
were shaped like hearts

she would crush me between them
wrap them round my waist
squeeze and laugh
invite me to escape
which I never could

her face screwed up with the effort

ankles crossed at my back
thighs scissoring
kidneys crushed

incredible pressure

I feel it still

BIG BROTHER

they bicker
snipe
parade their hatred
gossip
bitch
reduce themselves to marrow
rats
autocoprophagic
not my specie
not my specie

did they hear the bombs explode
did they smell the blood and
hear the screams

they're what we've earned
they're what we've won

PACK UP YOUR TROUBLES

the old people gather
in their medals

below the fly-past
tell stories of old battles

within smelling distance
of the bodies rotting
on the bus
& in the three tunnels

there is talk of wounds so huge
that working organs were exposed
of faces burnt away
of limbless torsos
of seeing a ribcage on the pavement

there is talk of 55,000,000 dead
worldwide
30,000 or so in London alone

the main words used are
terror &
defiance
terror & defiance

a lady weeps

there are figures moving through dust
photographed faces
appear on lamp-posts & railings
& the word there is
MISSING
exact body count will not be known
until the bits are fixed together

the survivors still gather

London born from blood

smile smile smile

DURING A TYPING BREAK

I think how hideous it would be
to be left in this vile & confusing world
without you

summerflies bash their brains on the panes
spin & buzz
then do it all again
because they are alone
in this wormbent & frying
world without you

high buzzards squeal in the bright high blue
baby slow-worms hunt slugs in the greens
I recall a weeping woman
alone on an underground station somewhere

in Barcelona they sleep in the sun
on raw stone benches
at the end of the road a bus farts smoke
upstairs my computer hums in waiting
& I would hate to be alone
on this dignity-less spinning foul ball in the sky
without you

some iced vodka
the football results
a garden in flower
& I could bless your drunken soul

hearts await
& lungs await
& fingertips await
& don't leave me on this whirling wild &
crazed planet
this fucked-up ugly lovely world
this teeming screaming world
without you

ah, bless your drunken soul

RED BERRIES

I see the little bluetits on the trellis
from the bathroom window
as I'm taking a piss

winter
is dragging itself over the mountain
& it has driven the birds down here
to seek the red berries
& the peanuts that I put out

for a reason unknown
they make me think, these little birds
of those times
when, in a dark & dirty kitchen
I had nothing
but a pen & some paper
& a potato baking in the oven
(if I had gas)

& a fire inside
a blue, blue flame
that I didn't know how to use or douse

I remember the rain lashing on the windows
& I remember the emptiness
of that kitchen
& the dark unlit rooms in the flat behind me
& the big empty bed waiting
& the tiny black-&-white TV

& these birds now take me back to that place
at that time
on their golden fluttering wings
when I had fuck all
& wanted nothing
else

DON'T LET ME FALL

sometimes
all it takes is a phrase
as the TV burbles in the next room
as the sparrows squabble
in the lane
as four hours away
an afternoon promises
alcoholic oblivion

all it takes is a phrase
& you're back on a boat in Greenland
chipping ice from a berg
watching the seals roll

you're back convulsing
under a pub table
in a northern city

you're among the standing stones
of Ales Stenar

observing the tarantulas
in Spain
the heat an assault

in a Canadian kaleidoscope
of snow snow snow

just one phrase
unbidden & unknown

but you suddenly know
completely know

that all this will die
with you

FEBRUARY 2006

None of us has ever
seen this snow before

the flakes of it
falling slant-wise
out of a sky turning blue

and behind it, inside it
the birds are still singing

we'll be in Belgrade this weekend
a strange and childish British couple
who will drink too much
and say peculiar things
and who will
sleep late in the hotel bed
and look around at the new city
in wonder
as we do now
at this February snow

remembering younger years
when it seemed to snow more
and a wonderful cat
who would dig warrens in the drifts

and now it's stopped
a snowfall
that lives as long as a poem

A HOOD TO HIDE YOUR FACE

I saw Belgrade in a blizzard
& once I had a cat

that knew when I was upset; he
would nuzzle my face
& hold my neck in his paws

I saw the tigers in their concrete enclosures
as I drank coffee & brandy
above them of a morning
& I thought of them loose in the city
when the zoo was bombed

& once I had a fine & powerful dog
who I sat with on a tiny island
for four hours
while the brown sea swayed around us

& once I remember wondering
what the fuck was happening to me
as I drank with a woman
on a promenade
watching the sun set

no sleep for 3 days
no food for 4
what was happening to me I thought
what the fuck was happening

I ate fish on the banks of the Danube
& drank good wine

& the mist of the world
fell slowly & to the left
the cold caps
began to dissolve

& once I stood on the bed of a drained
salt-water lake
lightning forking the ground
around me
& once I had a rat
who would sleep on my chest
as I slept on my back

& I remember the sun going down
as the world's gas sighed & hiccupped

I will see the sun rise now
as I Google *dead flowers*
as I Google *lonely horses*
& know that the mountain stays there
in the dark
as I Google *abandoned shoes*
in my small room
with the stars outside

THEN

I remember our shadows
slanting across the concrete slope
three of them
me my cousin and sister
and I said
it's a good job you've got a big boy to
look after you
and then bigger boys threw stones at us
and my sister said
you can't hurt us

he is five

DON'T CRY FOR ME COS I'M GOING AWAY

the dizzy spells are getting worse
skin crawling, heart going like bricks
in a cement mixer

I can see that hooded cunt
up in the tree-line
where the snow won't melt
until June

but the windows are lashed with rain
today
Tom Waits roars on the stereo
& I roar along with him

fists clenched

sober

but mighty on the earth

THE COBBLER'S DOWN THE COBBLED ALLEYWAY

By the side of the pub
is a cobbled alleyway

opposite the chippy
next to the French restaurant

it is dark & it is narrow
& it is overlooked
by fire escapes & high windows

& there are small buildings there
once stables I think
& one was once a shoe-mender's
where I would take my boots
whenever the soles flapped from the uppers
to be nailed back together

boots that belonged to an ex-girlfriend's
grandfather
motorbike boots
from WW2

cleated & buckled I loved them
they had stamped on Nazi faces

I was wearing them
when I had sex down that alleyway
with another woman

drunk one mid-afternoon
but we were interrupted
by someone running down the
fire escape
clatter clatter

I withdrew
we zipped up
& ran

the cobbler's closed down
at the same time
that I began to make money
& didn't need his services anymore
because I could buy new boots

which meant that I could throw
the old ones away
so I did
& I was sad
because I liked those boots
they had stamped on Nazi faces

but I could afford new ones
which wouldn't break
which wouldn't come apart

now the alleyway is empty only
sometimes there is a puker
down there
& maybe a hidden copulating couple
I don't know
I don't go down there anymore
I have no need to do so

POETRY

There was a moment -
when he was about 18 -
when he stepped outside of himself

& saw himself
on his knees
naked
his arms around the waist of a standing girl
also naked
his face pressed to her flat tummy
her looking down sadly at the top of his head
& holding that head in her hands

& he remembers that moment
two decades later
and thinks how he'd like to re-create it now
in paints
or pastels
or charcoal
or better still
in a woodcut

but
alas
he never learned the skills
in the intervening years nor
he sometimes thinks
any others

DROUGHT

no money no money
as the grass browns
and the trees gasp

and the taxman holds his hand out
and the bank snaps for its mortgage

and the sun scorches it all away

and at the weekend
four days ago
I walked through a house of slumbering middle-aged men
saw bald patches and beards
empty bottles and mirrors mottled with powder
and the mountains mooned green around
under a blue blue sky

and the lakes dry out
and the reservoirs are salt

and I can't pay what I need to pay
and I don't know what to do

A HAPPY MEMORY

The blue-tongued skink
walked around the back garden
at the bottom of the fence,
his overlapping scales
like artichoke leaves
glistening in the sun ,
over the plot where we buried the cat
and over the burrow
where the giant spider once lived

the Australian sun
hit the Australian sand

I followed the lizard
on my hands and knees
so I could see him closely
and because my eyesight was bad

I scraped my knees and palms
on the hot sand and dry grass
but I got close to the blue-tongued skink
that hot day in western Australia
when I was ten years old

the next time
I sit trembling
in a psychiatrist's office
chewing the skin off my lips and teeth
drugs throbbing and humming in my veins
and he leans across his desk
and asks me for a happy memory
this is what I'll tell him:
Oz
the lizard
and a ten year old boy

OH MY GOODNESS, WHAT A PERFORMANCE, AND JUST LISTEN TO THAT CROWD

It's here, I say, I
tell them all that the burning is back

and that I'm about to embark
on a bout of creativity
that will last for a few years
and I'll write plays and novels and screenplays and essays and reviews

and here I am, gone 3 PM,
no work done except to bring
some notes down from upstairs
and place them on the table
where I can see them.

There is a film in the DVD player
and I will watch it
as soon as I put down
this pen.

Novels and plays and reviews and things, yes,
all these
lies.

But sometimes there's so much to do
that to start doing it
would tell you
of how vast the task is
so you just don't bother,

as ants continue to labyrinth
your garden,
slugs to eat the strawberries.

DO THIS AND YOU'LL FEEL BETTER

hold me under water till my face turns blue
paint a jolly roger on my hat, my shoe
count your racing heartbeat two-by-two

you bloom, as the world shrivels

get up early to sow your eyebrow oats
leave chicken entrails for the weasels and stoats
sail out to sea in a snot-green boat
you bloom, as the world shrivels

put wine in your car instead of oil
bury your spouse in six feet of soil
jog on the spot til your gonads boil
you bloom, as the world shrivels

plug all the gaps so it can't get through
there's a chasm above you, plug that too
become an exhibit at the zoo
you bloom as the whole world shrivels

LET ME GO FIRST

don't be sad
when the leaves show their veins
don't be sad
when the little birds stop visiting
because
I would miss you
with an agony that crippled
& I would greet each morning
with a gasp of disbelief
at the horror awaiting

& don't be sad
when there's only one towel
drying on the rail

& don't be sad
at the breadcrumbs hardened to gravel
because I would wish my life away
every waking hour
& I would pray
that there would be no more of those

so no don't be sad
because I think I will be happy
at last

DRAINED

there's a hole in my heart
    where the rain gets in
and a hole in my head
    where the money goes

not the babbling of daytime tv
    or the clicking of computers
    or the boiling of a kettle
can drown out the hiss of that downpour

it opens on waking
    and overflows on sleeping
and I ask it to close
or drain itself
quietly
    so its gurgling won't wake my girlfriend

sometimes there's a voice inside it
    distant but discernible
and it promises

that it'll never close
fully
that it'll forever remain
    slightly ajar
and not always
    is that voice horrible

I tell it that
    I know these things
that ten tons of earth
    a landfill
will never staunch it
    so to check its hunger
but it doesn't seem to heed these words

it yawns open
    in Wales
    in New York
    and at new year
it sucks rain into it
    during drinking
    and sex

and I have tried to ignore it
and I succeed half-way
    only when I weep
    and yes of course I fucking weep

like everybody

SPRING MORNING

It seems that all the good
is coming undone -

smoking now banned in public places
drunkenness a disease
that needs to be addressed
sex made leering,
obscene,
a sin.

We work for this.
We give our peace and security
in promise of a calm
that is never allowed to come

and you might lie there
in bed
one fine spring morning
with the sunlight pouring
across your windowsill
and the alarm shrieking your dreams away
and your first thought on waking
could be:
Bring flames.

TYPE 2 DIABETES

I am losing sensation in my feet
blood sugars plummet
I can no longer drink like I used to

I can no longer fuck like I used to
but I try.

Tosches has the same problem
H.G. Wells did too
and I wonder why the flame of your fingertip
chose to sear
my pancreas

I wonder how furred my arteries are
if I'll go blind
if I'll lose my legs
sightless crab man

Jeffrey Barnard
legless in a wheelchair
ordering gin by telephone

pushing 80 at his death
a long time off still
comfortably distant

but the story from here
ends with you
rushing into the room
because I'm screaming your name

A GRIEF THAT HASN'T HAPPENED YET

that toxic blood from the radio
the spawn on the walls
the sky's blue high-heeled boots

will all make sense

no more will the shower hiss
no more will the bed rock with panic
and me and the mouse
and me and the sparrows
and me and the frog that eats the slugs
will wonder no more

all exhaust will be benediction
money could be dipped into soft-boiled eggs
geese will form the letter L
and the warplanes will trail the ribbon of
the old typewriter I used to use
that lacked several letters

all the bricks I lived within
all the slates I raged beneath
every blade of grass I trampled
every last, lost drop of brine
I'll find in my pockets

beetles will be gentle fellows
crabs will coax from under rocks
in their envelopes of blackness
the horizon's islands will not sink
and the mountains won't be blue

alcohol will burn no longer
socks will heal themselves
pimples will pop with suicide

countless hearts will thud thud thud
swallows will roll with the summer

sewers gurgle
hospitals snigger
I'll skin my knees with toasted muffins
wear asparagus
look for and find unconcern

dream of the falcon that I dreamed in the womb
find carpet burns meaningful
scrape the mortar from between the bricks
so that all the walls fall down

mosquitoes will find me irresistible
the moon will turn bright red
and I won't forget to put flowers on your grave

EX

I lived for drugs
I fucking loved drugs
I felt complete when I had drugs
I dreamed about drugs
I yearned for drugs
there were drugs in my knees and elbows and eyes
blood-drugs
tear drugs
grope-light at 4AM
and birdsong at 5:30
I loved my sickness
adored my disease
and now I love the spiders,
and the blue-steel-skin
of mackerel

only just dead.

ONE QUESTION AND AN ANSWER

Q: why did you give me
   the kind of mind
   that feels the
   terror of death
   so very very
   keenly?

A: because if I didn't
   your heart
   wouldn't have soared
   like a condor
   this morning at 10AM
   when the gleaming
   green beetle
   crawled across your hand.

HERE ENDETH

you don't look for God's blueprint
in your own diabetes
or your girlfriend's alopecia
or whatever vile tumour

seethes in future days

you look for it
in your own anger and disgust
and nausea
at that absence

once, I was four years old
and I looked at my own shadow
slanting, elongated
up a concrete embankment
and I knew then
that I'd never forget the image

BANKS OF FOG LIKE BIG WHITE PILLOWS

And they say that, when you're in love,
there's nothing you need be afraid of,
but that's not true – there are tumours
and car-crashes and furious strangers,
more worry & fear than ever,
& the knowledge of the price we pay for love
in no way lessens the expense.
Ah, well, on this blue day, there are
some good gifts, maybe, some fine things
which, if you let them, might captain
your soul; the day has arms
with which to gently squeeze
the sickness out of your ears.
Throbbing veins on your legs & blemishes
on your toes & this, yes, is lambing
season; they run & spring in the fields,

collared doves roost & chuckle
on telegraph poles & I know that the
mountain behind the house
& the ringed ancient fort below it
would happily snare my eye,
& I have stared into the face of a lion,
I have seen whales breach around icebergs,
I have been saved a thousand times over
yet remain as lost as an unbaptised child,
sitting at a table I never thought I'd have
in the failing health I thought
would never desert me. There are fish
in the lake & lizards under the stones
& soon the opposite of ice will rise,
hawks in the trees, badgers in the burrows,
banks of fog like big white pillows
we'll yearn to rest on forever,
which we'll do, separately or together
or maybe not at all. The mystery
of this & the magic of this
& the rolling promise of that fog
tightens around your skull like barbed wire.
If you stand by a river, you won't jump in;
if you stand on a mountaintop, you won't leap off;
but there'll be a name you'll call,
always the same name,
& you'll continue to call it even though
you might never receive an answer.

BOMBAY INSOMNIA

It's 5 AM. I haven't
slept. I've forgotten how
to sleep. Whenever I close

my eyes my brain becomes Bosch
and the consciousness of needing to sleep,
trying to sleep, ensures that I
won't. Sleep is impossible. Racing
brain. I stand at the window
beneath the aircon, its
whirr and coolness, and smoke
and feel the heat in the window glass
on my face; out there, below
in the crazed city, insane
city, pariah dogs sleep in dusty
gutters and crows crash through
trees. Men wash their taxis
in front of the Ahmed Joo
Jewels and Curios and the Simon and
George cleaners. They're like me – they
can't sleep either. Strange, this,
that slumber should become an
enemy, here, so far from home. I
feel that there is a presence
in the room other than the woman
sleeping in the bed. I don't
feel safe. I feel afraid.
It is 5AM and still a heat-haze
rises from the filthy streets.
I could walk, maybe. I could
masturbate in the other room. I
could write something. Instead
I stand at the window
and stare and smoke and it's as if
the city is taking its revenge
yet I don't know what I've done wrong.

DON'T MARK ME

That's what I'd say, when
cheating with other women,
to those other women: don't
mark me – don't bite
        or scratch
        or slap, no
        bruises
        contusions
        teethmarks or
        lovebites.

Now, tho, I haven't
cheated in years, and don't
desire to do so,
so go ahead, here I am,
mark me: mangle
        maul
        manhandle
draw blood, draw purple,
lattice my back with scratches
as
no-one will see it
but you.

PENRHYNCOCH INSOMNIA

It skulked into my luggage and I
brought it back from India.
I am utterly fucking exhausted yet
sleep is entirely impossible. There

is something in my head
that will not be switched off
and will not let sleep drown it,
will not let itself be silenced
in unconsciousness, will jabber and
caper and rage. The bedroom is a dungeon.
The mountain rises up behind the house
and is cold and dangerous and hates me.
My eyes are sandy. My mouth is dry.
I am going fucking insane.
Anxiety hovers and will avalanche,
smother and smash and I am useless
everything I have ever done is pointless
I am a smear on the earth
a shit-stain on the earth because I
just cannot sleep

TEMAZEPAM

If I have to take these forever
I don't care.

Little white pills. Small
circular friends, such
comfort here, the world
almost rights itself,

I have hope again
a form of happiness
again

bed is a sigh to slip into,
protection once more from the wind inside

little white pills
you are mine

SEPTEMBER AFTERNOON

Thunder frenzies the local dogs
& lightning skeletons
the ridge's trees.
In ten days
I'll be 42. It'll
still be raining.
Medication & philosophy have made
the fear recede,
the anxieties & insomnia have gone
with the headaches & the
dizziness
& death is an acceptable necessity,
waiting all those years away,
in the rumbling flashes of
salt-white light &
water falling.
At these times
you know & appreciate
the one & simple, single rule: to
feel every second of life,
record every heartbeat, every blink,
let the skin thrill
in every living instant,
& sustain that til the very end,
the final throb, just before
the eyes close and the chest settles,
the final nano-second

before the lights go out
feel that, fuck, *feel* it.
Ah, the stink of ozone is here,
& I see the lakes on the mountain
above the roof,
tall lightning leaping their black waters,
the birds silent in the pines
& with rounded breasts
& alert eyes. In ten
days I'll be 42.
A sense of continuity returns – that,
after I've left the world,
when all is dead,
there will be something left alive,
& why would you advise a cripple
to cast aside the crutch?
The sky's hot artillery
illuminates it all,
the thunder rumbles within, &
in the rain we are all a-drench.
People die. People
eventually have to die, because
each raindrop transports a
hunched homunculus, huddled
& expectant, as early biologists
imagined sperm to do.
And so the dogs bark. And so
I'll soon be 42,
magpie on the wire,
I tell you I'll be 42
& I never thought I'd live this long
but listen to me, chatternag,
today, with all the billion tiny
people falling, I'm so very very

glad that I have.

TUESDAY NOV 11TH: REMEMBRANCE DAY, 2008: 90 YEARS AFTER THE ARMISTICE

It's the way the little things amass,
the thousand little things
that clamour to be bought, to be
in your life: cat litter, cat food,
washing-up liquid, hand soap,
light bulbs.

Then there's food.
Then there's tobacco.
Then there's anti-depressants
and other medications
and alcohol and books and continued shelter
and the things which, the way you live, the
way you are, don't have to be hunted for
like love.

Yes, well. Minutes pass in silence.
The red flowers bloom,
in fields and on lapels.

The culture continues to strive
to turn us into shells or fools
and the many million murdered in the mud
spin the world with their turning
and the meaning of life
and the meaning of death
and the meaning of creation
grow little trees

from their rotting.

Yes, well. Winter comes in,
hauls itself over the mountain.
In Australia
the beaches bake
and the stars are unfamiliar
and bugles blow
and eyes ooze
and my cat sleeps on the sofa
with all the world in his crossed
small paws.

It goes on, this, it will always go on,
long after I've gone,
long after this flesh
has fertilised the flowers,
the fuses,
the fighting ants
and my muscles now cry out for exercise.

Such ugliness.
Such massive movement.
A universe in each red petal
a God in each petal hell or heaven

and there's bleach, soap, bubble-bath,
pens and paper, petrol,
milk.

IT'S MORE OKAY THAN IT'S EVER BEEN, SOMETIMES, LIKE RIGHT NOW

I love my cat.
When I lie supine to read,

he sleeps on my chest,
the image of bliss,
sometimes grabs my arm
in his sickled paws,
the arm that he's scabbed and shredded,
and licks the skin with long rasps
as a lion licks the neck
of a dead antelope.

It might be because I recently
saw something
that resembled hell, I believe.
A hell in this life; unbearable
existence
but the endless trapped horror
of being dead
even worse,
and the ever-present terror
and the crawling in the skin
and the sleeplessness

there was no exit.
All of that gone, now.

One day my cat will die
and I'll bury him
and weep over his grave
and play celebratory music
and get drunk
and if he lives to an old age
I'll be old myself,
if I live to an old age too
and am
not captured first.

But I love my cat.
I like his swagger.
I like his ferocity.
Still kitten, this weekend he can leave the house
and be a little leopard in the long grass.

That one day all this will end.
That one day all this will
be no more to me
means only
to feel and to fight and to seethe
and be, every fucking second, breathing
on the earth.

In this country
at this time of year
it is dark at 5PM.
An hour ago
the sun settling beyond the hill
over the sea
tickled the walls of my room
with fingers long and pink,
golden thunder-light
threatening storm.
They say it will freeze this weekend.
It's Wednesday now.
I like writing in this notebook
at the table
as the TV burbles in my ear
and I like the cheese sandwich
I am about to eat
and the tea
I am about to drink

and the rolled cigarette
I will later smoke
and I like the hacking and scabbing
on my arms
and I love the cat
that has made those marks.
The world
spins in my head, as
it always has.

TOOTHPASTE

One night
in bed
we talked
and both agreed that
we'd like there to be
another flavour; herb or
aniseed
or something. Mint, you said,
gets boring.

Next day
you came back from the shops
smiling and you said
lemon and you took a tube of something
out of your pocket.

Fifteen years ago, this was.
Last month, I chose from
bubblegum
chocolate lime
basil
fennel

germolene.

On the box it had a smiling citrus
and the words: *a lemon-fresh
taste that lingers.*

Fifteen years.
They knew something that
I didn't, then.

'I KNOW I'M ODD'

he said, & I can do nothing
but trace the sharp ridges of my toenails
& bite my fingernails to bloody rawness
&
wonder at the small birdlife
in the hedgerow & garden.

I can do nothing
but sleep for half an hour
around 3 in the afternoon
& admire my cat
& guess at the grave
& becoming something else
& how
& when
that will happen
but I do understand the why.

I can do nothing
but brush my teeth
& cook simple food

& regard the moon from my pillow.

Ah, well, no; I can also
come to an acceptance
of myself
whilst getting slowly but deeply
drunk
on a weekday afternoon
in a bar
in Prague.

STILL & SMALL, STILL & SMALL

there's a little voice
& it's in the birds – if I
listen hard
I can hear words, buts of phrases:
here, & how, &
come again , & something
about joy

there's a little voice
& it's in the plants, the flowers
& the herbs & the grass – it
tells me about a world
beneath the soil   where death becomes
life   a movement towards light &
it tells me about
achingly slow dreams

there's a little voice
& it's in the stones

& what hides beneath them – it
talks about
the vitality & importance
of the faintest grey slice
of daylight

there's a little voice
& it's in my cat & all it says is
I am cat &
that's enough

there's a little voice
& it's in me – you
are dust, it says, your
body is dust
so while it's still flesh
coax it into doing what
no other dust can do

there's a little voice
& it's in everything around
one little voice with a billion tongues
& today they trill
out the only song that's ever mattered
the only song there's ever been

today

ON THE FOURTH OR FIFTH DAY OF KNOWING YOU

we sat in the beer-garden
of the Ring o' Bells pub

at a wooden table
under an umbrella
and the soft rain kept everyone else away

and we sat close
drinking
and touching and wondering
sheltered from the soft rain
our own circle of dryness
and we did not get wet

it was night-time
we were alone in the garden
discovering
beneath an umbrella

a gentle rain fell
and we did not get wet

A MOMENT TO GET MY BREATH BACK

a village
in the middle of quilting fields
white houses
red tile roofs or thatch
a church
a cemetery
a pub which sells cider and ale
and bread and cheese
with a beer garden behind
coloured by wings
various wings

a pond on a green

and in that village
a house
a cottage
without right-angles
and bursting with books
basked by cats
a garden full of
vegetables and flowers

and in that house
under the moon
under the sun
amongst the books
amongst the cats

me
happy

content to be waiting
with my scars
and bad insides

happy to be sitting there
smoking and sleeping
endlessly waiting
endlessly

AS ALWAYS, AS RARE

Our skin burnt.
We slept on beaches
and on boats

and in the car
overlooking mountains and bays.
We drank in pubs
so close to the sea
that our feet got wet
as we drank
and we spent entire days
by mountain lakes
talking and smoking and doing nothing much else
as our skin burnt
pink to red
then brown to
golden.

And now on August 28th
2003
this seems like a day
to break a drought -
the first sustained rain
in months.

I heard it whispering
on the window
this morning as I
lay in bed.

It surrounded me as I worked.

It drenched me
when I went to the shop
for milk
newspapers
tobacco.

So they're over again,
those long days in the sun,
those sandy sea-spray salty days
of alcohol
and slow movement
and wild sleeping,
the days of burning skin
are gone again.

And I'll tell you this: that,
sitting here
in this mortgaged kitchen
with food in the fridge
and an electricity supply
and tobacco to hand
and cleaned clothes drying in the airing cupboard
I am glad
of the rain.

ROBIN

I left stale bread
& cereal
out in the garden
but the crows came
& chased the small ones off -
the sparrows, the tits, the finches
even the starlings,
& the thrushes
seen off by the black barking birds
the inky-black screeching
birds of carrion.

But this morning in the rain

on this first day of autumn
I saw him,
his beak heavy with sodden bread,
his feathers wetly plastered,
labouring to lift himself
& his prize
on his saturated wings.

Splash of red in the deep green leaves.

I stared at him,
gazed at him,
in love with what he is.

INDELIBLE

On one side of the humpbacked bridge
the gouges in the tarmac
are still there.
Two yards long, deep dark
gouges in the tarmac.
You remember the sound of the car
as it made them; you
remember the lurch in your stomach
and how, as you were airborne,
you thought calmly
that you might die.
You remember the delirium.
The excitement of that flight,
that 80 mph
screaming approach to the bridge.
You remember that life was there to scrap.
You remember how young you were.
That the ugly future

could be caught and controlled
in wreckage, in endangerment,
could be improved
by the shriek of the car
landing on the slope of tarmac,
creating those gouges, those scars
that are still there, that you look at
every time
you return to that place.

'SOMETIMES I GET SUCH A FRIGHT'

Middle of the night & I'm awake.
Rain on the windows, the
barking
of a distant dog.

She is snoring.
I can't sleep.
I nudge her gently
& she shouts & kicks
& I reassure that nothing's wrong,
it's all okay, I just wanted her to
stop snoring.

She re-settles. Then her quiet voice
near me in the darkness:

sometimes I get such a fright.

Something snapped in me
because I know you do,
I know the frights that afflict you,
the oblivion in the grass, the air,

the fragility of our lives, loves,
togetherness, I know how these things
& the promise of their extinction
terrifies you,

& I know too
that to the gentle there should be peace
instead of those fears in
wet blackness

& I cannot bear the cruelty of that.
Sometimes I get such a fright.

Yet there is the warmth of you
within the winter,
the shared bewilderment,
the desperate worry
about black ice
& snowy roads

& that which will always bind us -
the lantern heart
the hearth heart
the frostberry heart
so snappable

never go.

LUST

burns
like eaten embers
gulped in buckets

screams
like wind
on the Pendam mountain

seethes
swampwater

battlefield bones

combusting guts
of a compost heap

bubbles
like Iceland's mud

pops
like suds

bursts
like a mosquito too blood-stuffed

hums
like flies on cowshit

buzzes like them too

roars like a combine harvester

snarls like a badger

soars like a buzzard
searching for prey

and like loss, like wonderment too

it never goes away

ARCHAEOLOGY

don't
dig in
the fertile
soil
unless
your heart
is a
spade

WHAT WE DO WITH TONGUES

she's down there
sucking your dick   your balls

your eyes are closed
your arms spread
cruciform

she surfaces, asks
if you're okay
& you say

yes & tell her that
there's a lot on your mind at the moment
it'll be alright
if she carries on

she descends again

ducks her head
you start to respond
in that lovely warmth

your groans are a different language
unspellable words meaning
loss
& shattering

a new tongue
that tells of nothing
but broken hearts
that never heal

GIVING UP SMOKING

wheeze -
fold clothes -
masturbate -
read – but don't take -
anything in -
scratch -
walk -
hoover a carpet -
that isn't dirty -
see yourself -
as a non-smoker – and
fail – fail -
reflect that – the best
people – tend to be smokers -
and remember -
Canada -

try to write -
with your brain -
spinning -
unfocussed -
without nicotine -
pick at a scab -
eat that scab -
gaze -
gasp -
bite fingernails -
bite toenails -
dread eating -
drink water
drink water
drink water -
think of the people -
thousands of them -
it would be pleasant -
to – punch -
pull grey hairs -
from head -
chest -
check -
face in the mirror -
for new wrinkles -
and -
at midnight -
drive – the 8 mile round trip -
to the 24 hour garage -
buy a 10 pack -
light -
inhaaaaaale -
feel -
oh so happy -

again -
fuck it-
fuck it

MORE THAN HALF IN STUPID LOVE

there will be a garden
at the foot of a blue mountain

it will be evening
a setting sun

there will be drowsy bees
and darting bats

I will sit with whiskey
and books

in that garden
with a table-cloth pure white

all history
sleeping in my veins

and there will be no more fighting
within

no more objection
no

not even for
the thing that will tumble down off the mountain

out of the redness
of the sinking sun

and from inside the house
a woman's voice will be calling my name

and I will lean back
smiling

regret nothing
look up one last time

at the night's first
glittering star

and gladly offer it
whatever light

I might
have left

ALMOST IMPERCEPTIBLE

The delicate tickle on my back
pulled me from sleep; tar-dark,
blind completely,
something softly fluttering

against my bare back,
some shadowy, felty thing
detached
from the outer dark
and come in through the window
to tug me up from sleep.

A shrug and it was gone; I heard
its wings
whirring
in the blackness of the room.

And the moment will come
when a shrug will not remove it,
that midnight intruder,
when it will rip itself
from the black blankness
and seek me out
alight on my body
not to pull me up out of sleep
but to drag me
further under.

TWO SHADES LIGHTER THAN DIJON MUSTARD

so blue the sea, so clear blue
that when I came out of it the blue
stuck to me

I escaped the heat
in the stone hut
to eat fish
and drink cold clear water
and Croatia crackled outside

the cramps began
half-way through the tuna
terrible, crippling
doubled over in physical pain

I squinted and limped
back out into the heat
and climbed up through it
through that beauty
up the hill above the bay
cramping, awful
picking up pieces of tissue
only to reveal old and stinking lumps
of fly-blown human shit

I squatted behind a bush
groaned, dropped the shorts
and let it all out

the bowels collapsed open
and sprayed greeny-brown shit
all over that landscape

as the sun sizzled
and cicadas chirped

how amazingly good it felt
to cover that place in liquid shit
to know that others

had done it too

I went back to the beach
and the hut
to eat more fish and drink more wine
the cramps all gone
having shat all over that beauty

my stink now
part of that sea
that mountain

had to let it out
had to
no choice

what else could I do
but shit all over that wonderful place
like so many others
had done before

A LESSON IN GRAMMAR

because sometimes
the caribou
do not migrate in the proximity of the wolves
does that mean

they kill more wolves
than wolves do caribou

because many wolves
starve to death

because a mother wolf
must eat a cub
then puke it back up
into the mouth
of its brother

because her mate
might travel 10,000 kilometres
and never find the caribou
and will himself
starve to death

and when I was at school
I was taught one thing -
to never start a sentence
with *and* or *but* or *because*

and it meant very little
when I was a boy

but it means
even less now

AS CLOSE AS WE MAY EVER COME

on a day like today
you know that there is nothing to say
but you find a way
of saying it

the doctor tells you you're ill
diabetic
yet you feel as strong as an ox
and anyway you're taking the pills

it's all so unimportant
it's all without resonance
you dig and delve and hope to discover
but nothing reveals itself,
nothing sounds

on a day like today
there is nothing to say
yet you still
find a way of saying it

THURSDAY

it's like a veil, up there,
the mist on the mountains above the village
like a veil
the world has pulled over itself
to hide its face from shame

last night
a friend told you
that when he was a child
he was raped by his father

last weekend

you visited a friend in hospital

she fell off a cliff
six weeks ago
and she is shattered

broken woman
turned child-like by her injuries
told you that she thinks
it may have been a suicide attempt
although she can't properly remember

last night you were drunk
and you'll be drunk tomorrow
you are a type 2 diabetic
a depressive and a pisshead

it's Thursday, that's all it is

LLANBERIS PASS

snow still streaks the peak
of Yr Wyddfa

it is early April yet
the air hums with spring

above the nearby mountains
rise bigger peaks
and bigger peaks again
one of them
the tallest
whiter than the others

you remember
standing on that peak
and trembling at the view
the world so far below you
so small
and you even tinier
a raindrop in cloud
somewhere so high
above it all

and this is why you drink
this is why god burns
painfully

this is why he joy of being alive
is so strong
that it sometimes feels like
an ache too great to bear

today
on the Llanberis Pass
you decide not to leave the car

APRIL, END OF

the lambs are filling out fast
& soon will not be lambs

behind & beneath the breeze

is a dry heat
concocting sweat
under my fleece

my part of the planet
spins
towards the sun

& I think of lakes & lager
of sleeping on shores
of peeling skin & the taste of salt
& a pleasing sandpaper face

soon we will look out over estuaries
soon this pain in my groin will go away

soon I will have to shun concrete
& lie bare-backed
on dewy grass

soon I will break melons on tree-stumps
& make my face sticky
with their juice

the time when we will move
from the shade of packed pine woods
& stare blinking at the sun

is not at all
far away

RECALLED

mortar splits in the sun
& bricks crumble like pastry,
releasing a million ants
each one
wearing a yellow hard hat
& each one
waving a flag
emblazoned with a swordfish
as swordfish themselves
leap in the harbour
around the boats
in which
purple light in the shape of a farmer
sets sail
plots a course
for the golden
horizon

A PRESENT

I never expected it to be easy
but nor did I think it would be this hard,
weeping at 9:45 AM,
coffee and tobacco
& the whites whirring in the washing machine,

bees buzzing in the bush beyond
the door
left open for the spring,
sun's here & flower blossom
& the smell from the rosemary,
that catch in the chest
& the heat in the face
& the tears falling as the body jerks with
sobs.

The bus rumbles up the road
ready to take people over the hill
into the town
& can hear birds in the trees
& the cockerel clucking in next door's garden
& people's voices
as they pass up the lane
& I can see my skin prickling into pimples
as the sadness runs through my arms.

Never easy, I thought,
but not this difficult,
after Barcelona & before
everything else,
that big forest
I've been lost in forever
& all the methods tried
to escape it
useless now, lost, & never workable anyway,
but mid-morning reached
with brine & nicotine
& the urge to die,
I never expected this, no, nor
thought that it could be.

ROOM SERVICE

this is how it often goes – you
get off the train
or plane
or out of the car,
find the hotel in the unfamiliar city,
check in,
drink a few in the bar
then go to the room
with bladder bursting
but nothing works – no lights
no water
no air-conditioning -
you must install your door-card
in a box
or call the front desk
or something

then
when you do have water
it's too hot or too cold
or the TV won't work
or something
some little thing

& after the reading
in the bar or restaurant or at the party
you'll drink until you reach
that ecstatic distance

from everyone around you,
a state
you're always chasing
& how different that will be
from pissing in the darkness
or burning your knob & balls
in the needles of burning water
how different
that will be from
everything here

LINES WRITTEN AFTER VISITING TINTERN ABBEY

I sat in the cloister
& watched the sun slant down
through the windows
that once held glass
& the middle-aged couple came in,
heard
before seen
because he was shouting at her, screaming almost,
something about it being
her fault
that they were lost
or without food or drink,
some matter
easily rectified.
The female half
didn't respond, except to purse her lips tighter
& clutch her bag harder to her chest
& follow him deeper

into the ruined abbey.
His voice
& its insane anger
bounced off the broken walls,
circled the columns like the doves & pigeons
but utterly without
their grace.

Wordsworth, I thought,
like me,
you know fuck all.

SQUAWK

The crows are at it again -
all day it seems
they have perched on the telephone wires
to make their puzzling noises

they woke me up at 6AM
& now 12 twelve hours later
they're still at it
untiring, unending, unflagging

what are they saying to each other
what questions are they asking
what answers are they giving

triangular on that wire
like bunting arranged
for a demonic wedding
thousands of voices

throbbing through their feet

these inky-feathered eavesdroppers
black against the summer blue
squawking, humming
squawking, humming

a million mysterious mutterings
sinister
such soundtrack to a Tuesday

ABOUT TEN PAST THREE, MAYBE

she was ill with
flu
on the couch in her robe
& I sat on the floor
at her bare feet
& I said
you look beautiful

I don't feel like it she said
but it was true
she did – the sweats
from her skin
had turned that skin darker
had clumped her hair
with grease
& made it look thicker
blacker wilder
and in that white towelling dressing gown. . .

she did she looked
truly beautiful

ten years ago or so
& why I remember it now
peeling potatoes in the kitchen
another woman out at work
 my 36th birthday
two days away

why I remember that moment now
I don't know
I don't know
just one instant on this sojourn
just one moment in this mucky junket
one pointless point
of wonder

WHITE FLAG

We'll be OK
&
we'll buy a house
with a mountain view
a blue mountain view
& we'll live there

with a cat & a dog

we'll have a vegetable patch
& some fruit trees
& we'll grow our food
beneath the blue mountain

during winter nights
we'll sit by the fire
& hold each other
drink tea & watch films
read
& tell each other stories

foxes will visit the garden
badgers
hedgehogs
bats & birds of prey

maybe we'll keep chickens
for their eggs

I will cook you
slow pots of stew
& make you laugh
when you come home

we'll sleep together
in a big soft bed
& we'll walk together
up the big blue mountain

on summer evenings
we'll sit in the garden

drinking gin & tonic
vodka & orange
cold beer
as fish roast
on the barbecue

& we'll look out at
the big blue mountain

& talk fondly
of the time
when our circumstances
were just a conversation
a poem and
a dream

WORKING GIRL

I am in a pub in Shrewsbury
drinking with a whore from Birmingham.
It's nearly 6 o clock, the hour
of rush & happy.
The pub is old, wooden-beamed,
the bar a splash of ordered light
in the maroon gloom
& the town outside the leaded windows
is busy & beeping.
The woman is big & blonde
& we drink together
& lean into each other's words,
we talk about the weather
& her job.

We talk about Britain
& her job.
She makes me laugh
& her make-up crinkles around crow's feet
& she says she has to return to work
soon, the red door with the brass 8
underneath the railway bridge.
There are towels tacked over the windows.

There is another planet here.
She will not tell me
any details
only that she's saving up
to study for a degree.
Only that she doesn't mind her job
because it's a mere
means to an end.

There is another life-form here.
I must leave to catch a train.
I give her ten pounds
& kiss her powdery cheek
& leave the pub, into the traffic,
seeing my face in glass
drunk
sagging
somewhat red
& the coldness of the station platform
is like a face,
the face you have now you're growing into
& that you really never wanted

DAFT TERRY MULLIGAN

They let us out of the cells
around 4:30 in the morning
outside the bridewell
in the cold city dawn
we lit cigarettes.

I complained that the cell was freezing
& that the bench had been too hard
to sleep on.

Not mine, he said; my cell had
soft walls, like cushions. On
the floor & ceiling as well.

I looked at him & he didn't smile,
just blew smoke towards the Mersey.

Well, I suppose we're all good at
something, aren't we? Got
at least one talent. All
of us.

HARD SKY

That winter
the frost took the strawberries
& the slugs ate the lettuce,
so cold & sudden early winter
& the amazingly hardy red berries
became by the morning just

black mush. &
late that night
with woodsmoke in our clothes
we took whisky & cigars
outside into the cold & hard & dark dark
world
& watched the spider spin its web -
so beautiful, that spider
in the porch-light, the green & black
of her thorax & legs
& the assiduity of her architecture.
We watched her build as we shivered
& then returned inside
to the flames. &
I went back to Wales
through a mist so thick
& scaled & sea-smelling
& when I awoke the next morning
that mist was in my flat; the
sofa, the TV, the furniture
all vague & ghostly
in that thick wet mist. It
was like living elsewhere,
it was like being else – me
waving my arms
to clear the housebound fog,
that veiled invader, like
that spider not at all.

NEW HOUSE 1

The reek of paint

among the boxes - &

she is somewhere
because I can hear her voice

never thought a life
could accrue such luggage

never thought a life
could come to this

some happiness
amongst the wreckage

although a type of that
has led to this -

remember
the ruins
& see the resurrection

our walls
our roof

our curry bubbling on our hob

our paint
our mess

see what life we have made
& how far we have come

from chaos
all the way

to chaos

we love it &
it is ours
when once
nothing was

NEW HOUSE 2

You wake up & it's
still there. The
beams the wall, the
roof it's all still here &
although it's been
almost laughably
upsetting (nothing
works) you
find yourself happy
to wake up in it &

30 years are removed from your life -
you're 6 years old again, un-
sullied, excited, nothing
works but so much fucking space

& just this little miracle – that
it's still here &
so are you

NEW HOUSE 3

& it's ours now, we've marked it,

our colours our books our smells,
years stretch ahead & we'll walk
within these walls we'll
pace this floor &
stare at the ceiling &
out of the windows.
The jets scream overhead
& the whole valley pulses
with their passing, the
air throbs & crackles & they excrete
heat, drop it like soft bombs. The
crows flap as they split the sky
& songbirds bauble the hedgerows
& yesterday a buzzard wheeled squealing
over next door's garden & caused
the chickens to cower. It is
all world, it is all one place
like & unlike a hundred others
& like them it too will end; but
slugs leave trails on the beer bottles
in the garden & two flies bounce
against the bathroom window
& have been doing so for days.
Earlier I rescued one; he
was sluggish on the draining board,
ugly & pathetic, so I coaxed
him onto a piece of paper & threw
him out into the night. It is
all world, yes, it is all one place, &
I remember the space
each side of Crib Goch,
falling away so far into nothingness.

SIMPLICITY

these unexpected joys

a bowl of strawberries
a pot of tea
on a hangover

& on the TV
Laurel & Hardy

triple bill

it is perfect

FAME ACADEMY, 2003

This is us, here – the desire to be
something
anything else,
to hope that in the gaze lies some transport
or a way out of slavery
& that we have
made that for ourselves, that juggernaut
judgement
of what we are being what we do
& who can sneer
at the heart repulsed?
Who can deride
the rejecting soul?
Only the crow on the fencepost,
only the cat at the top of the stairs

who seems to smile
as behind him the sun sinks
behind the trees
& behind them, the mountain.
It is all we are.
It is all we do.
Turn the TV off & see yourself reflected
in the blank screen; it's only
the contrast caused
by the other, brighter colours
that makes it appear black.

HIS LITTLE 'HELLO' NOISES

The feral cat enters the bedroom
around 4 in the morning
decorates the darkness
with his trills &
chirrups

I hear him settle himself
under my side of the bed

I reach under & touch fur
he beats my fingers with his wet paws
& begins to purr

we share many things
the cat & I
no words written for months
now
hear me purr

OKAY

I'll look handsome in my coffin.
They'll do a good job at
patching up the wounds; the powder
on the bruises, the stitches,
they'll replace the missing teeth,
they'll put me in a collar & tie
to disguise the massive gash.
The glass eye will be convincing,
although my eyes will be calmly closed.
The wig will cover not just the baldness
but also the sections of bared & shining skullbone
& the fingers, laced across the chest,
will have been straightened & re-set
& false fingernails glued onto the beds.
Cotton wool in the mouth
will fill out the hollows
made by the shattered cheekbones
& a latex implant
will replace the smashed chin.
Lipstick will disguise
the blueness &
rouge the black.
There'll be stubble.
My eyebrows will be trimmed.
There'll be no expression at all on my face &
I'll look handsome in my coffin.

TICKS

there was that one in my leg
in Australia
when I ran away from home
& lived inside a tree for two days
that had been hollowed by lightning

I gouged him with a sharpened stick
& pulled until he came out
but his head stayed in
burrowing
& still I have the scar
a purple blotch

there were the ones on the bullocks
I looked after
fed & cleaned out
& coaxed into the truck
that would take them to slaughter

one animal
had them all around his eyes
a constellation
around a deep & grieving moon

there was the one I wrote about
in my second novel
& discovered more things about them
than I ever knew because
by this time
there was the internet

there were the two
on the tiny feral kitten I took in

hanging grapes on his flank
in the silver fur
the vet twisted them out
& they dragged their stuffed bodies
across his worktop
he burst one with a thumbnail
& out came blood

there was the one
on the cat that the kitten now is
it's a scab I said
you said it's got legs
I twisted it out
it was already dead
the Frontline had killed it

& lastly there was another one
on the same cat
still alive
but poisoned by the chemicals
the cat was treated with
it
stumbled towards the bread-board
you crushed it in a tissue

my leg itched
I bent to scratch it
remembering that first one
thirty years ago

suck our blood
suck my blood

tick tick tick tick tick

TWINS

And my heart did thump
I mean hard, like,
and she said is there anything else
you need to know and I said
do you love me a huge lot
and she laughed
and told me to not forget
to post the keys through the door
and she left for work
and I turned over in her bed
found a cool spot on the pillow
and went back to sleep.

So many years between then and now.
Last I heard she is the mother
of twins, not babies anymore.

I AM FULL OF LIFE

they said don't trust him he'll
steal your money he'll try it on
with your wife or girlfriend

he'll drink every drop of
alcohol you have in the house they
said he can't be trusted he's a

burden a liability you don't know
what he's going to do next

but
when he was in the sea
he had no such worries
there in the waving weed
in the ocean
the water he had no need
for such fripperies
he had everything when
he was in the sea watched &
witnessed by the
stalk eyes of crabs
moved by the current & only
that singing down the centuries &
across the wet acres through
the ravines over the sunken
mountains the endless plains

the slashes of light & the
bioluminescence for his lantern
he had everything he did when
he was in the water he did
not need your shirt or
your booze or your money

A LOT LESS OFTEN NOW BUT STILL THEY COME

that time
in the late-night mini-mart
in Cambridge

I was at the booze shelves
you were at the tins
I heard a deep voice

turned to see you smiling
over the top of the shelf
at a huge Rasta guy
so I went over to you
& he said you look after her mon
she is one special ting

his voice rumbled like a train
I know, I said
& we bought our stuff
& left

nearly two decades ago &
you have children now &
I have a house & a healed heart
& a career that I picked at & plucked at
when I was with you
for a while it seemed like a dream
but
it doesn't anymore

it was cider I took home
tuna it was, I think,
for you
probably in brine

LITTLE BIT OF A SING-SONG

Are you sad?
Yes I'm sad.
You look sad. Why are you sad?
Because I haven't seen my cat for 3 months & I think he must be dead.
Is that all?
It's enough. I loved him. He was my totem.
No, I mean, is there anything else?
Yes.
Such as?
I've just finished writing a novel.
Isn't that good? I'd be celebrating.
But now a crutch has gone. I feel unmoored & adrift & alone.
So start writing another.
I will. But I need to mourn first.
Mourn?
Yes. Because the last novel, the one just finished, was an elegy. A long elegy.
For what?
Your soul.
My soul?
The collective soul of the species that we both belong to.
Is it sick, do you think?
It's dead. Dead & flown & you are hollow shells.
What makes you think that?
Because of the things I've seen. The things I've done. Your blood is hate & self-regard.
I don't hate anyone.
Yes you do. You're not being honest.
Well, that's a lot to be sad about.
It is. And my cat has gone.

Well, I'm hungry.
So am I. Let's go get a curry.

SPECIAL DELIVERY

My postman died 4 days ago
said today's local paper.
Collapsed on his round, in the village,
said the local paper.
45 years old. A wife,
two daughters
said the local paper.

I never knew him really
but he was part of the world, part I'd
see almost every day,
to nod to
wave to
accept parcels from; books,
brilliant cheques, fan-mail,
subscribed-to-magazines,
birthday cards, Christmas cards,
bills, invoices,
packets & parcels & envelopes.
We'd smile at each other.
I'd thank him & he'd nod okay.
At Christmas
I'd give him a tenner.
Of course there were bills
& other missives of misery
but I'd wait
for the sound of his van's engine

rumbling in the lane.
There'll be more packets & parcels & envelopes
but the hands that deliver them
will be unfamiliar,
the village my world
is unfamiliar,
uncertain & trembling
as if plates are shifting
beneath it.
My postman is dead.
I didn't know him
but I knew him well.
Postie,
dead too young, your wife a widow,
your children father-less,
here's something small back
from a man
who didn't know you
but who you made, on several, many,
occasions,
very happy.

THAT STUPID CLUB

It was the weekend
of the massacre in Norway
& the lonely going of you.
Anders Breivik, become manure,
but Winehouse, Winehouse -
if that was me
at your age
I would never have seen

Breivik's eyes
I would never have seen
all those other things
& I never had your voice
but it had
me & many others.
There is a hand
that seems to snatch
certain ones – that reaches out
from the rivers the concrete
at that age, or thereabouts.
And I would've gone tooth
pretty & bruised
& I think
tonight
when nothing is wrong
that I missed my chance
the river didn't want me
as I was,
pretty & bruised,
having achieved nothing
but
having done everything.

NEW WORLD

My tomcat is lapping the bathwater
his pink tongue
at my nipple

he thinks of leaping on
the isle of my belly
then decides against it

one of his sisters joins him
on the slippery edge

they are black & sleek & muscled
they have claws & teeth
I have testicles

I pull the plug
& stand, wet
& the cats
study the slurp of sudsy water
vanishing clockwise
northern hemisphere
as they are

FACEBOOK

There is an empty dress
that once you looked so pretty in

there is a burst of yellow
from the daffodils
early blooming daffodils
this winter has been mild

yet there is a frost tonight
& sharp dark air
& stars like hanging blades

heat from the oven
heat from the bathwater

sharp stars & cold cold air
& an empty dress
that once you looked so pretty in

BINGE

I'd started at 11AM
& 6 hours later was
still going at it alone &
here they came
for the swift ones on the way home they
stood at the bar loud &
serious in their dirty
clothes & rigger boots &
the cement dust in their hair

of course manual work &
drinking are each as serious a
business as the other

one young one
told an older one
about the male friend of
his girlfriend I gathered
that they'd been spending
too much time together
it's catch 22 the old one said
do you smack him or don't you
the young one looked down
into his pint

my clothes were clean but

I knew the feel of filthy jeans on
clammy legs on
freezing winter mornings &
the grit in the eyes
& the thirst

I watched them the
labourers have their three that
turned into four make their
phonecalls & go
leaving puddles of dust
on the carpet at the fruit-machine
& on the strip of wood flooring
anterior to the bar

I watched them all go &
I stayed in my clean clothes
& skin & hair & never-ending
unquenchable thirst

JARVIS COCKER STOLE MY AUDIENCE

some festival somewhere
mud & beanburgers
weedsmoke wellies
fucking jugglers & self-delusion

& I went on stage
& saw all those faces
I was pleased & surprised

then some twat
put his head through the flap, said
for those of you who don't know
Jarvis Cocker's just starting his set
on Stage 2

it was an exodus
in a nano-second
leaving only people
I'd worked with or slept with
except my current girlfriend
but
she'd heard me bellow a thousand times
& Cocker only once

well
they'll always prefer his art
to mine I suppose
and there are multitudes here
& at least I got a title
that sounds like the title
of one of Jarvis Cocker's own
songs

ST FRANCIS OF ASSASSINS

The world gave me three kittens
tiny feral spitting
barely weaned
recently blind
said: they are now yours
to feed
& protect
& keep warm & safe

until they grow into tiny tigers
with rumbling in their breasts

the world gave me a moth
with feathers on its head
golden dust on its wings
a miracle
said: cup it as gently as you can
when you return it to the night

the world gave me a spider
trembling on his stilts
said: be certain his legs
all of them
are inside the rim of the glass
before you slide the postcard from Sitges
underneath

then the world
gave me a baby bird
unable to fly
loud in his peeping
& told me to
feed him with milk & crushed woodlice
a blob of this
on the end of a matchstick
every two hours
throughout the night
until he can whirr
around the room
at which point
you will leave a window open

the world then gave me a mole

on the kitchen floor
with a coat of felt
& clawed spades for hands
said: let him go in the field
& ignore his biting
because the blood from you
is not important

and then as it must the world gave me a man
finds his fun in death
finds a short relief
in the extinction of life
& told me to
stay away from him
avoid him
disdain him
condemn him
because he seeks to destroy
that which gives you joy
that can still the storm
for a moment

he has a hole inside
that needs to slurp into it
the things
that make you happy
for a moment
so keep him at a distance
avoid avoid
 say *fuck you*
should you meet him
fuck you, you cunt

& hold your hands out
in the halo

WE COULD BE OUTLAWS, JUST LIKE WE PLANNED

I hear that
you've been in and out of rehab
for the past twenty years
that you've lost your kids
and your husband and your home
and that
in the town where you now live
you're known
as the jakey, the alcoholic tramp
asleep in gardens not yours
in sheds not yours
raving at nothing in the public places

and they were wild times weren't they
drunk on milk and whiskey
when we spoke about climbing trees with rifles
and picking the cunts off
one by fucking one

FORTUITOUSNESS

Lucky, & luckily, for a poet,
'morning' sounds the same
with a 'u',
the worm has the same shape as

a snake
as a penis,
Liverpool's two cathedrals
are linked by a street called Hope
etcetera
etcetera
& so on.

None of this matters, of course, or,
rather, matters far less
than
thinking of this last night
as sleep rolled into me
& the owls called outside the window,
I had a cat to touch
& a warm woman to hold
as I looked forwards to
mourning.

YOUNG

It feels like I'm dying, I said,
it feels like death,
& you kicked me & cried
but all it was
was
I was coming down from speed,
& we spoke about small dogs
running in their sleep
& I hadn't slept

& I mentioned something about
you taking a boat trip
after my death
& looking into the eyes of a dolphin
& knowing it was me.

Blame the amphetamine,
but of course I'm sorry
that you cried, that I made
you cry,
& along with this
there were
the imprints of cat's paws
in the snow outside the kitchen
we held each other in
& both of us on a crumbling castle wall
you never used drugs like I did
nor drank like I did
& maybe that's why I think of you now; the
summer arriving
the swallows returned
temporarily sober I am
& something like happy or at least
not sad.
All those years, all those years
steam
like that in the kitchen
boiling potatoes the kitchen we
held each other in
with snow on the ground outside.

I'LL SEE YOU WHEN I SEE YOU

In the trembling light
when I was too drunk to see anything
except
your anger & disappointment

in the sea
with the sunlight
striping your back

on the castle wall
with your eyes all alight

on your back on the bed in
the caravan

topaz
it shone all topaz

on your knees above me
your hands drumming against the wall

above the tins of tuna &
below the flicker of fluorescents

& like I never was to see you
welcoming me off a train
or in the expectant queue
at arrivals

but then
there you'll be
your hair waving like weed
when

for the last time
I slide beneath the waves

MORE SHAME

Make it cheap,
let it be cheap,
the kind that catches in the throat
& starts the bile to churn

let there be bruises
& bad teeth
a disease, maybe
trackmarks
& a history of loss & maltreatment
dizzying to be told of

make all the alleyways stink of piss
& let all the drugs be dirty
let the nostrils be rimmed with red
& the whites of the eyes
any colour but white

let there be violence
to each other
& tears
let there be encrustations & scabs

bitterness & resentment
& an aggression seething
neighbour to hatred

let backs & bellies be battlefields
on which
to fight our wars
against ourselves

let there be pleading
& fury
broken glass & stained formica

it will be
needed & feared
like the wolf when I was a boy
how he wailed & snarled & grumbled
as I stroked him

my hand tiny in his mane
through the bars of his cage
his massive skull
rubbing against my fingers

hating himself
for needing it so

& powerless to do anything
other
than drift towards the bars
where the boy stood there waiting
& reaching out to him

FOUR DAYS AND COUNTING

I still don't like you
& I never will
to me you are scum

the very worst that my species
is capable of

but

sobriety van be binged on like any
intoxicant;
more, the mind says,
always more,
reading in bed
anticipating dreams
& waking
anticipating the quick
horn-lock with the world
in each grunt of which is a word
in a good order

and this is what it is – I was
a desolate, descending dickhead
a familiar condition but one which, here,
with my half-wild cat on my knee,
his claws in my arm,
the skull sharp & clear,
the heart knowing what it longs for &
the lungs knowing how to find it,
each day a feast & each night-time a choir,
the muscles rising to the surface,
the drugs & the bottles & the women & the weeping
already beginning to fade,
the bird's thoughts so near,
the sap of the grass in the blood,
the distance & acceptance of dying,
the last death of it all,
is as far removed from me as those

little-England idiots
that live on Gibraltar.

BAD NIGHT

Primo Levi escaped the death camp
& started his war
with freedom

I told my mother
that I hoped the lump on my chest was malignant
cos then I'd soon be free of this shit

woken by the sweat on a dribble down my back
a warm & rumbling presence on my thighs
that was a cat

something sounded outside
a whooping grunt
& then again the dribbling sweat

I told my mother
that I wasn't happy at her house
& only felt relaxed & settled
when away from my family

& then the dribbling sweat again
the screech of the alarm
the woman leaping on me
to awaken

half-naked
warm breasts in my face

a rough fucking night
but into a good morning

SOME-FUCKING-THING

Work work
Shanora Pandora
& the storks left Britain
a long time ago
but I've seen them, I have,
on the twin chimneys in Estonia

Daz died alone with the
needle still in his arm
Charlotte swinging from the beam
taking away from herself & the world
what the cancer had left

beavers back on these islands
& wolves, they say
don't tell me how the story ends
but let everyone play in the dust

fresh from the shower
& sweat dribbling down my arms
& yesterday on the wall
outside the front door
a wolf spider crouched over her eggs
but she wasn't there at dusk

work, work

Shanora Pandora
I recall very clearly
that first hit of smack
& what happened to me after the vomiting

watching the storm
behind the mountain
the sheets of lightning
a series of low concussions distant

play in the dust just
play in the dust nothing
can grow in it
anymore

NOT QUITE MUSHROOMS

Every fucking poet has got one about fungus;
mushrooms or toadstools or mould, how they
grow towards the light, lean towards the light,
& I remember the growths
that appeared overnight behind the cistern,
up the mildewed wall,
small relatives of the plate fungus
on fallen trees in the forests.

Like pasta shells, she said; we
can eat them with tomato sauce & cheese.

They stayed there & spread for a few days
then I took a spoon & a sheet of newspaper
into the bathroom, scraped them away
& they fell touched my hand: dead
skin: flesh: spongiform & resilient
like cheap cheddar
horrible
a thing that nobody but an embalmer
should ever have to feel
against their skin

& there was a smell, like
spew like
rancid cheese.

We moved out soon after that,
into an even cheaper place, so whether the pasta
re-grew up the mildewed wall
behind the seeping cistern
I do not know.

But I knew I would've stayed there
had I been allowed; maybe not forever, no,
but certainly for longer.

That's my thing about mushrooms; that's my thing
about fungus.

MOUSE

The cat brought in a mouse, alive,
crazed wee thing, dropped him
& he

scampered up onto the edge of my laptop
& began to lecture me about time;
he quoted Nietzsche, Marvell, John Donne,
Buddha Confucius Socrates Christ,
told me that time runs by
incredibly fast
& that fangs & claws await.
I told him to fuck off; you're a mouse,
I said,
go & preach to other mice,
& besides,
what do you think I'm doing with my time?
Wasting it?
Fact is, I was putting down brilliant words
in a brilliant order
before you came in & started prattling on.
The cat watched, licked her lips; such green fire
in them eyes.
I wrapped the mouse in a fist; he
tried to bite but could only pinch,
just could not break the skin with his tiny
jaws, his tiny teeth, &
I
took him outside & let him go in the hedge
where I deposit the cat's corpses,
those presents
less lucky
than this gobshite of a thing.
I
went back inside.
The laptop hummed.
My other cat had brought in a bird, & there were
feathers fucking everywhere,
brown tipped by black -

a sparrow, then.

REGRET

If she knew
but she doesn't know
if they went
but they won't go
because power loves power & this will not end
& this is the world

when I build
& don't destroy
& disinter
in the man the boy
& cease to grieve before the thing is dead
I am the world

it's freezing cold
the sparrows fall
comes from nowhere
microscopically small
bursts so big that eats the sky
& I am the world

screaming rupture
spewing out blood
stamp it under-
ground all good
more more more more more more more
& this is the world

beseech it seek it
then throw it away
not good enough
anyway
cos you love your life as you try to die
& this is the world

cover it in concrete
as you can
fight it fuck it
shadowman
the night-time's in you the moment you wake
& I am the world
this is the world
Christ what a cunt I can be

IN A VALLEY OUTSIDE CRICKHOWELL

dozy dogs and brilliant women
robin hops, cocks, sings
booms from further down the valley
as some little-dicked pricks kill birds

february still and we're outside
me and the women and the dogs
only contrails across the flat blue
and the shadows spider-leg fine

there is cheese and tea and bread and hangovers

dozy dogs and brilliant women
ruins on the wooded hills
in which impossible lives were lived

it is we agree like spring there are
no daffodils as yet
shoots only thin green spears
in the woods on the hills with the ruins in them

one woman has flown a glider over the himalayas
another has known ayahuasca in the jungles of peru
another has seen hospitals and jails and the sun rise in chicago
with me with me with me

with every boom these women
flinch and sneer and sigh
the dozing dogs twitch
and the robin falls quiet

I burst an orange in my biceps
showing off to make them laugh
the river is a constant gurgle
a raven croaks nearby

dozing dogs and brilliant women
first food outside of the year
long and lazy and lovely but boom
as some pin-dicked pricks kill birds

SHARED HOUSE

I sucked your tits
you sucked my dick
I licked your cunt
you licked my balls
I penetrated thee
in orifices three
when I came
I came on your face
when you came
you crushed my skull

in the morning
when you came back
from the kitchen
with tea and toast
you accused me of using
your margarine

CHICAGO

a blade of wind it is said
scythes through the city in the colder months
across the water is one more state
and the emails are lost in the ether

and of course it won't be forever
there's a beautiful woman who proves true to the heart
it'll last as long as the wheels come down
and thud on an earth not this

always diarrhoea in Illinois

some germ in the water of the lake
from hovel to hills to horror to here
and the texts say something about loneliness

and of course it won't last forever
a beautiful woman has proved true to the heart
it'll last as long as the wheels come down
and thud on an earth not this

pink and green and pink and green
casino and cocktail lounge they said
feet could sink in the carpets and there was
whisky to rid the taste of gin

and no it won't last forever
a beautiful woman who proves true to the heart
it'll last as long as the wheels come down
and thud on an earth not this

from the railway girders above came rust
the scabs and flakes in the curls
look at that face a mistake don't make
and it can't last from the 88th floor
don't say 'me', never say 'me'
the airliners rise and they sink beneath
across the water is another state
look down look down don't look down

and of course it won't last forever
a beautiful woman's proved true to the heart
it'll last as long as the wheels come down
and then thud on an earth not this

A HAPPENING

Hold me tight again,
like you never did, in that
hotel room; don't tell me once more

about the people in the other rooms,
the sex and arguments they were having,
their dreams;

don't hold me again
in the warm afternoon breeze
bringing car-horns and sirens

through the lightly flapping curtain
and call the front desk
for more wine.

Go through with me again, like you never
did, what the coming night promised;
the food and the drink and the sex,

how we would dance
beneath the palm trees
on the marble promenade,

the salt air off the sea
in the folds of your white dress
presenting your brown knees,

and the voices around us in a language
neither of us understood.

Don't hold me again

on the marble promenade
in the warm salt air
and don't gaze with me up at the mountains

that surround the city,
and out over the bay
where the islands aren't.

Let's stay here, you never said, I like it here.
And you never spoke the words
let's never go back again.

"Griffiths' language is lyrical, brutal and startling ..."
The Guardian

"Niall Griffiths poems are true, relentless, unnerving, offbeat and beautiful - with just a touch of blood."
Jenni Fagan

£12.00